Cyrus Kingsbury Remington

A Record of Battery I, First N. Y. Light Artillery Vols.

Otherwise known as Wiedrich's Battry, during the War of the Rebellion, 1861-'65

Cyrus Kingsbury Remington

A Record of Battery I, First N. Y. Light Artillery Vols.
Otherwise known as Wiedrich's Battry, during the War of the Rebellion, 1861-'65

ISBN/EAN: 9783337116026

Printed in Europe, USA, Canada, Australia, Japan

Cover: Foto ©ninafisch / pixelio.de

More available books at **www.hansebooks.com**

SURVIVORS OF BATTERY I, FIRST NEW YORK LIGHT ARTILLERY.

Dedication of their Monument on East Cemetery Hill, Gettysburg, May 20th, 1889.

From a Photo. by W. H. Tipton.

A RECORD

OF

Battery I, First N. Y. Light Artillery Vols.

OTHERWISE KNOWN AS

WIEDRICH'S BATTERY

DURING THE

WAR OF THE REBELLION, 1861–'65.

THIS BATTERY PARTICIPATED IN OVER FIFTY ENGAGEMENTS AND BATTLES DURING ITS PERIOD OF ENLISTMENT, MOST NOTABLE OF WHICH WERE THOSE OF CROSS KEYS, THE SECOND BULL RUN, CHANCELLORSVILLE, GETTYSBURG, LOOKOUT MOUNTAIN, RESACA, KENNESAW MOUNTAIN, CULP'S FARM, ATLANTA, ETC., ETC., CULMINATING AT RALEIGH, N. C., WHEN GEN. JOSEPH E. JOHNSTON SURRENDERED TO GEN. WILLIAM TECUMSEH SHERMAN.

IT WAS THE ONLY SEPARATE COMMAND ACTIVELY ENGAGED, REPRESENTING THE CITY OF BUFFALO, IN THE BATTLE OF GETTYSBURG, JULY 1, 2 AND 3, 1863, WHERE IT HELD THE IMPORTANT POSITION ON EAST CEMETERY HILL, AND WAS MAINLY INSTRUMENTAL IN CHECKING AND DEFEATING THE CELEBRATED CHARGE OF THE "LOUISIANA TIGERS," AT THAT POINT, ON THE EVENING OF THE SECOND OF JULY.

COMPILED FROM RELIABLE SOURCES

BY CYRUS KINGSBURY REMINGTON.

BUFFALO, N. Y.
PRESS OF THE COURIER COMPANY.
1891.

To the Memory

OF THOSE "WHO DIED UPON THE FIELD OF HONOR," AND
THEIR SURVIVING COMRADES OF

Battery I, First N. Y. Light Artillery Vols.

IN THE WAR OF THE REBELLION, WHO, IN COMMON WITH
OTHER PATRIOTS, SUFFERED GREAT HARDSHIPS
DURING THAT EVENTFUL PERIOD,

This Record,

WHICH HAS BEEN FOR THE COMPILER A LABOR OF
LOVE, IS AFFECTIONATELY INSCRIBED.

INTRODUCTION.

To the Surviving Members of Wiedrich's Battery:

In compliance with a promise made a short time since, I now present you with as full an account of the history of the Battery as I have been able to obtain; dating from its formation and incorporation into the service of the United States in 1861, to the mustering out in 1865.

It has been a peculiarly difficult organization for the historian to record, from the fact that the company was formed upon a *fighting* basis, and consequently the fame of its doings has only been heralded by those outside its membership; for during the full period of its enlistment,—three years,—there is not, as far as known to me, upon the records of the daily press of this city, with the exception of two or three letters to the *Democrat*, any communication from the company to the public, of the battles in which they were engaged; nor is mention made of the heroism of an individual member of the Battery. Such facts are, however, undoubtedly, on record, and will only require, in the future, some one to give them to the public. This is in contradistinction to the many letters printed from members of other military organizations sent from this city at that period. These do not militate as against such; on the contrary, if Wiedrich's Battery had had among its members a skillful writer, much historical matter would have been saved, and would have greatly facilitated the present pleasant task.*

* Since the above was written, Mr. Frederick Smith, of the Battery, has sent me an interesting memorandum kept by him during the famous "march to the sea." It is placed in at page 113.

In order to give you this meagre record, the files of the daily papers, for items; printed War Records of the Rebellion; the Report of the New York Board of Commissioners of Gettysburg Monuments; Story of the March to the Sea, by Maj. Nichols, of Gen. Sherman's staff; Gen. W. T. Sherman's full report of the march; Gen. H. V. N. Boynton in *United States Service Magazine;* Guides to Gettysburg; information from the lips of survivors, who, after a lapse of twenty-five or more years, are not expected to remember full details of those stirring days; and lastly, a personal examination of the famous battle-field of Gettysburg, has given the writer a realizing sense of its importance in the War of the Rebellion, and of the advantage gained there, in which was truly foreshadowed the " beginning of the end."

This little work is for the present use of the members. It is the intention to continue the gathering of material which may be embodied in a memorial volume, to be placed finally with others of a similar nature, in the archives of the Historical Society of this city.

BUFFALO, N. Y., February 16, 1891.

CONTENTS.

	PAGE.
RECORD OF WIEDRICH'S BATTERY,	9
BATTLE OF GETTYSBURG,	15–31
BATTLES NEAR CHATTANOOGA,	33
LAST ASSAULT AT CHICKAMAUGA,	37
ROSTER ARMY OF THE CUMBERLAND,	53
EXTRACTS FROM NOTES KEPT BY COL. WIEDRICH,	57
DEDICATION OF MONUMENT AT GETTYSBURG,	61–97
ADDRESS AT DEDICATION BY CYRUS K. REMINGTON,	79
THE HEIGHTS OF GETTYSBURG. RECITATION BY MISS NETTIE WIEDRICH,	82
RESTORATION. A POEM BY JEROME B. GREENE, M. D.	84
LIST OF SUBSCRIBERS TO DEDICATION FUND,	96
FIRST REUNION,	97
ADDRESS AT REUNION BY CYRUS K. REMINGTON,	99
LOOKOUT MOUNTAIN. RECITATION BY MISS NETTIE WIEDRICH,	107
SECOND REUNION,	112
EXTRACTS FROM NOTES KEPT BY SERGEANT SMITH,	113
ROSTER OF BATTERY I, FIRST NEW YORK LIGHT ARTILLERY (WIEDRICH'S BATTERY),	121
APPENDIX,	135

MICHAEL WIEDRICH,
Captain of Battery I, First New York Light Artillery.

THE NEW YORK
PUBLIC LIBRARY

ASTOR, LENOX AND
TILDEN FOUNDATIONS
R   L

A RECORD
OF
WIEDRICH'S BATTERY.

THE Act of Secession, as adopted by the Southern States, was made under the pretense that State Sovereignty was still a good plea for their attempt to withdraw from the Union and to maintain slavery; but, happily, that theory is now forever exploded. The United States of North America still exists, and will continue to if in the future, as in the past, every patriot will do his duty.

When President Lincoln made the call for 75,000 volunteers, the German element of our citizens were among the first in offering their services to the Government, and during the war following we had many distinguished foreigners with commands, notably Generals Schurz, Sigel, Steinwehr, Blenker, Willich, Osterhaus, De Trobriand and others, and many who did not attain to a command, but were conspicuous for bravery and self-denial; the latter are the heroes of unwritten history.

The Act of Secession by the South was consummated early in January, 1861, and on the 18th of the same month the Battery, commanded by Captain Michael Wiedrich, attached to the 65th Regiment, N. Y. S. Militia, this city, at a meeting held at the Armory, unanimously resolved to offer their services and hold themselves in readiness to serve their adopted country. Such resolutions were sent the Governor of this State, and in due course of time the following reply was received:

STATE OF NEW YORK, ADJUTANT-GENERAL'S OFFICE,
ALBANY, January 21, 1861.

CAPTAIN M. WIEDRICH, 65th Regt.:

Sir—The Commander-in-Chief directs me to thank you and your command for the tender of their services to aid in enforcing the laws and protecting the Union. Your letter of the 22d inst. informing him of such tender by a unanimous vote of the company, will be placed on file to be referred to if the services of the military of the State should be required for that purpose.

Yours, etc.,

D. CAMPBELL,
Assistant Adjutant-General.

When President-elect Lincoln passed through this city on his way to Washington, D. C., for his inauguration, this company was ready to be summoned for duty. On the day of his inauguration, March 4th, while the Battery was firing a salute in honor of the event, a member of the company was seriously injured by the premature discharge of one of the guns.

On the 26th of April, the Battery reported 100 men fit and ready for duty.

During the following months the men were actively engaged in perfecting arrangements and organization; but it was not until August 21st that the General Government sanctioned their request to be assigned to the command of Gen. Fremont, then in Missouri. Col. William P. Carlin, formerly of this city, and at that time in command at Pilot Knob, Mo., hearing of this decision, and knowing its commander well, forwarded an urgent request that the Battery be sent to him; this was not, however, to be, as on the 25th of October an imperative order was received from Albany, N. Y., to report immediately to Adj.-Gen. Hillhouse, at that place; and within twenty-four hours after the order had been received, the Battery was well on its way to the Capital. The promptness on the part of the Battery at the first, in offering their services, their readiness to depart at a few hours' notice, was one of the distinguishing characteristics which governed it through the long years that were to come to them as an organization.

The *Express* of October 25th, 1861, says:

Major Wiedrich received orders yesterday from Adj.-Gen. Hillhouse to report with his artillery company immediately at the Albany Military Depot. The company will accordingly leave our city this afternoon, taking the 5 P. M. train, New York Central road. It will start from the camp at Fort Porter, at 3 P. M., and march to the depot, attended by Miller's Band. We have not learned whether any of the home military organizations propose to tender an escort, but we sincerely trust that such an honor will be paid to the departing company, if the suddenness of its orders permit the making of arrangements. It certainly deserves a farewell demonstration of some sort, for no company has been raised here in which Buffalo can take more honest pride. It is composed of a splendid set of men, stout, intelligent, soldierly-looking German citizens, and has attained a proficiency in drill and experience in the handling of its artillery that fit it for immediate service in the field. It is undoubtedly destined for the seat of war at once, the order to Albany being manifestly a preliminary movement only, with view, perhaps, to perfect its equipment.

In the next issue appeared the following:

Captain Wiedrich's Company of Light Artillery left town yesterday afternoon under an escort by the Eagle Zouaves, under command of Adjutant Louis Krettner, and the Tigers, Captain J. F. Ernst, Jr. The parade was very fine, and the departing company made a superb appearance. They are a noble body of men— every one every inch a soldier. The Zouaves had preceded to Fort Porter, and escorted the company to Niagara square, where the escort was joined by the Tigers on the right, thus proceeding through the principal streets to the depot. On leaving, those remaining gave the departing troops three hearty cheers and a tiger.

The next day's issue of the Rochester *Democrat*, in noticing the passage of the Battery through that city, said:

They are a splendid-looking lot of men, all hale and hearty, most of them above medium size. Many have seen active service in Europe, and will be found to be good soldiers in America. The company occupies two cars and are accompanied by a fine military band. The train remained fifteen or twenty minutes in the depot and they seized the opportunity to give some of the songs of the Fatherland, which were rendered with fine effect in the spacious depot. They sang in German three pieces, which were received with applause. They passed out of the depot still singing, which was drowned by the cheers of those who witnessed their departure.

Upon arriving at Albany they went into camp preparatory to being called upon for active service.

While in Albany, in November, they acted as escort, upon their arrival, to the Stoneman Cavalry Regiment, which was recruited in Chautauqua County, under the immediate supervision of George Stoneman, a native of that vicinity, and who afterwards became famous as a cavalry officer, and after the war was Governor of California.

November 15th the Battery left for Washington by the Hudson River steamers *Hendrick Hudson* and *Knickerbocker*, accompanied by artillery recruited at Rochester, Lockport and Syracuse. Arriving at Washington the Battery was attached to Gen. Blenker's division, and remained in camp at that place during the winter. In the following December they were ordered to Hunter's Chapel in Virginia.

Their "baptism by fire" was at Cross Keys, on June 8th, in which engagement they suffered a loss of three killed and six wounded. Thence they went to the Rappahannock, where at Waterloo Bridge, August 22d, they lost one killed and three wounded. At White Sulphur Springs, Warrentown and other places, they were always "where duty called them." And on August 30th, at the second Bull Run, they sustained

JACOB SCHENKELBERGER,
Lieutenant Battery I, First New York Light Artillery.

THE NEW YORK
PUBLIC LIBRARY

ASTOR, LENOX AND
TILDEN FOUNDATIONS
R   L

a great loss, thirteen men being wounded besides Lieut. Jacob Schenkelberger, who was deprived of one of his legs. The same shot struck Sergt. William I. Moeller, taking off one of his arms.

Mr. Moeller informs the writer that as he lay upon the field wounded he was taken prisoner by the Confederates, and that his wound was not properly dressed until eight days after; he was paroled, and for a long time was in the hospital at Washington, D. C.

In this engagement the Battery was almost entirely disabled; one gun only out of the six was fit for duty and several of the carriages had to be left upon the field, but by desperate exertions the disabled guns were rescued. The company was so completely used up, as to necessitate their returning to Washington for recuperation and new outfit.

Although not taking an active part in the Battle of Fredericksburg, they were there under Gen. Burnside, in position on the line of skirmishers, and eventually fell back in good order upon Gordonsville.

On May 2d, the next year, at Chancellorsville, the Battery again made a good record, and when compelled to fall back were obliged to leave two of their guns, one of which had been limbered up ready for removal—at one gun all the men had been disabled but one; 47 men were wounded and four of their horses killed.

The official account, as given by Captain Wiedrich, of the action at Chancellorsville, is as follows:

CAMP NEAR STAFFORD COURT HOUSE,
May 10, 1863.

SIR—I have the honor to forward the following report of the part taken by my Battery in the action on the evening of May 2d inst.

Late in the evening of the 30th ult. we arrived near Dawdell's Tavern, when I was directed by Col. Buschbeck, commanding 1st

Brigade, to take a position south of the plank road leading from Fredericksburg to Gordonsville, joining with his brigade. On the evening of May 1st I received orders from Maj.-Gen. Howard to place one section of my Battery in rear of his headquarters, which I did. When, on the evening of the 2d, the firing commenced on our right we were for some time prevented from opening fire; first, on account of the thick woods some distance in front of the Battery, which prevented us from getting sight of the enemy; second, when the enemy got in sight, our infantry while retiring rushed in such masses in front and past the Battery, prevented us for some time in opening fire, but as soon as the infantry were out of our way opened with canister with good effect and checked the advance of the enemy for a short time, but he soon advanced again and in greater numbers. Seeing that they were getting in our left flank I gave the order to limber up and retire; in the act of limbering all the cannoneers but one of one piece were wounded, and we were compelled to leave it on the field; and on another, after being limbered and in the act of driving away, the three horses and one saddle horse were killed and we were obliged to leave this gun also; on another two horses were killed, but by the exertion and good behavior of the men we succeeded in bringing it off with two horses only.

In this action I had one man killed, ten wounded and two missing. We retired to near White House, where I refitted the remainder of the Battery as well as I could for further action.

I am happy to say that all officers and men behaved well during the engagement.

Very respectfully your obedient servant,

M. WIEDRICH,

Captain.

Brig.-Gen. A. VON STEINWEHR, Com'g 2d Div., 11th Corps.

Only occasional official reports of the several actions in which the Battery was engaged have been at our disposal; such have been inserted in as nearly the proper places as possible.

If we are obliged to recount the old story of the Battle of Gettysburg, in which this Battery played an important part, those who wish may pass it over, but they must recollect that the contest at that place was an important factor in, or turning point of, the war; also, that we are writing for those who come after us. We are recording events which lovers of this country cannot read too often.

Gen. Hooker being obliged to give way before the advance of Gen. Lee of the Confederates, a stand was made at or near the village of Gettysburg, where during the three memorable days of July the Battery made for itself a name for stubborn bravery that will be appreciated more as the years pass by; it was at Cemetery Hill that the Battery was posted after the first day's fight and the death of Gen. Reynolds, and was in Steinwehr's division of Howard's Corps, with Geary's division of Slocum's Corps upon their right, resting upon Culp's and Wolf's Hills, that they helped successfully to repel Early's division of Ewell's Corps.

In order to understand more clearly the situation of the Battle of Gettysburg, we will go back to the 30th of June, when the First Corps of infantry, not exceeding 8,000 men, under Gen. Reynolds and the Eleventh Corps under Howard, encamped on the right bank of Marsh Creek, four miles southwest of Gettysburg. The Confederates, Hill's Corps of three divisions, namely: Heath's 10,000, Pender's 10,000, and Anderson's 15,000, were moved to the vicinity of Marsh Creek. The same day Longstreet's Corps followed, consisting of McLaw's 12,000, Hood's 12,000, whilst Pickett's of 7,000 was delayed in order to protect the rear and the wagon-trains. Two divisions of Ewell's Corps, namely, Rodes' and Early's, 10,000 and 9,000 men respectively, encamped nine miles from the village, while Johnson's 12,000 were at Carlisle. Thus were situated on the 30th of June, 29,000 men of the Union, and those named above of the Confederates, ready at a short notice to engage in deadly conflict.

At 9.30 A. M., July 1st, skirmishing began between Buford's dismounted cavalry and the Confederates, and at 10 A. M. the artillery was brought into action. Half an hour later the First Corps under Gen. Reynolds arrived and his men moved over the fields from Emmitsburg, and rested under cover of Seminary Hill. The extreme right rested on the Chambersburg turnpike, the left on the Hagerstown road. For two hours these 8,000 men opposed the powerful force brought to bear against them, two to one, but were enabled to hold their own and beat back the enemy in its fearful charges. It soon became apparent that our right was the main object of the enemy's attack. At 10 A. M. the division of Rodes and Early moved within a short distance of our right, forming in a suitable manner in a valley, under cover of a hill, for the purpose of supporting Heath, and of making a flank movement on our force. Rodes' division being in advance entered the fight at noon; Early at 2 P. M. Our small force being hard pressed were about to give way on our right, when a portion of the Eleventh Corps, which had been detained, came to its support. At 1 P. M. Schurz and Barlow's division passed through the town, and took position on our extreme right. By this timely support the tide of battle was stayed until Early's division was engaged. The other division of the Eleventh Corps under Gen. Steinwehr, by the forethought of Gen. Howard, was at once sent forward to occupy Cemetery Hill, at the south of the town; here the infantry and artillery, including Wiedrich's, did such faithful work that to them may be attributed in a degree the favorable results of the following days.

After Early's division had entered the fight it became evident that our right would be turned, and that we must either retire, be killed, or captured, as it was evident that the first two divisions of the Eleventh Corps, amounting to about 18,000 men, could not stand before the 40,000 of Heath, Pender, Rodes and Early. Gen. Howard, therefore, anticipating the natural result of this, had ordered the heavy artillery to be removed to the position on Cemetery Hill and a proper disposition of Steinwehr's division with a view to the support and protection of our retiring columns, and as the pressure of the advancing column of the enemy became great, our force was obliged to yield. The First Corps fell back and took position on the left and rear of Steinwehr, and the Eleventh passed through Baltimore street to the Hill, in front and on the right center. Being crowded in passing through the streets of the village, and being unable to repel the enemy, as a consequence 2,000 of our men were made prisoners. In the beginning of the engagement, west of the Seminary Hills, Gen. Reynolds, as stated, fell a victim to the rifle of a sharpshooter of the enemy. After his fall Gen. Doubleday assumed the command until the arrival of Gen. Howard, about 11 A. M.

The duration of the first day's fight was from 9.30 A. M. to 4 P. M., and our killed and wounded exceeded that of the enemy. They were encouraged and proclaimed it a victory, but, considering the disparity of numbers and condition of our men, they had little reason to boast. Ewell's Corps occupied the town, forming a line southeasterly to Rock Creek. Rodes' division lay on their right, west to Seminary Hill; Early on the southeast, and Johnston, arriving Thursday, forming the extreme left to the east. Hill's Corps were in position on the Seminary Ridge as follows: On the left was Heath, next Pender, then Anderson; on the right was McLaw's and Hood's division of Longstreet's Corps. This was the position of the Confederate force, July 2d.

It had been reported that when the Confederates had been informed that their Gen. Archer with 1,500 men had been taken prisoners, they replied: "To-morrow we will take all those back again; and having already taken 5,000 (!) prisoners of you to-day, we will take the balance of your men to-morrow." Having been well fed and rested, they were in good spirits, and were assured that success awaited their efforts on the morrow.

You may, therefore, imagine the feelings of our little band, which as yet consisted of only two corps; without reinforcements it would seem as though they might make good their boast. While our brave boys were retreating through the town all was confusion, but when they fell into position upon the Cemetery range of hills, and found themselves supported by the battle lines of Steinwehr, and a sufficiency of artillery in place, of which Wiedrich's formed a portion, then they had the satisfaction of seeing their late pursuers brought to a stand by the raking fire from these lines on the hill.

Gen. Lee's (Confederate) position at daybreak on the 2d day of July was as follows:

Gen. Ewell's entire corps was drawn up on the battle-field, with Johnson on the left, resting on Rock Creek, upon Benner's Hill; Gen. Early in the center, facing the ridge which connects Culp's Hill with Cemetery Hill; Gen. Rodes on the right, at the foot of Cemetery Hill, his main force occupying the town of Gettysburg, while his right formed a connection with the Third Corps on Seminary Ridge.

Gen. Slocum arrived with the Twelfth Corps before midnight, and upon him developed the chief command, until the arrival of Gen. Meade early the next morning, who approved of the action of Gen. Howard in the selection of their position. Gen. Slocum then placed his corps on the right flank; the second division under Gen. Geary on Culp's Hill; the first under Williams near Spangler's Spring; and the third across Rock Creek to Wolf Hill.

The Third Corps, Gen. Sickles, arrived shortly after, and at 6 A. M. came Gen. Hancock with the Second and the Reserved Artillery. Gen. Sickles moved his corps to the extreme left of our line, resting on the ridge just north of Round Top, known as Little Round Top. In the afternoon came the balance of the Fifth Corps under Gen. Sykes, and two brigades of the Pennsylvania Reserves under Gen. Crawford. Later on came the Sixth Corps under Gen. Sedgwick, with Lockwood's brigade of Maryland troops.

The arrival of these several corps was noticed by the Confederates, and they began to think that the prospects were not so cheery as they had anticipated; for they commenced to erect barricades in the village streets, and to remove obstacles that would hinder the advance of their forces, for they perceived that hard work was upon them.

The morning of July 2d was pleasant, the air was calm and the sun shone mildly through a hazy atmosphere, and nothing suggested the sanguinary struggles that were to close the day. During the early part of the day the enemy had remained comparatively quiet for the purpose of perfecting his plan, but about 4 P. M. they began the contest by opening a terrific artillery fire upon our guns, and immediately after by an infantry attack upon our left.

Suspecting, from some indication, that the enemy intended an attack at this point, Gen. Sickles prepared to frustrate the scheme. As the cannonading became general along our left and center, responded to by the one hundred or more guns of the enemy from Seminary Ridge and the hills to the east, Sickles' Corps, supported by a portion of the Second, with a determination to meet and engage the advancing enemy, encountered them on the Emmitsburg road near Sherfy's peach-orchard, and engaged them in a terrific struggle. Both fought with a determination to win, and at last Sickles' men began to give way. Rallied by him in person they arrested the advancing column for a short time, but finding themselves opposed by an overwhelming mass of the enemy, comprising Anderson and McLaw's division of about 26,000 men, they gave way.

This was a very critical period for us, as the point aimed at by the enemy was to break our left and flank us. This they would have been enabled to do if the Fifth Corps of Gen. Sykes had not at this juncture been brought into action from the Taneytown road at Sherfy's peach-orchard, and passing to the north of Little Round Top. So desperate were the Confederates, notwithstanding this and other re-enforcements that were sent from our right, they came near being successful. The enemy having driven our men before them were endeavoring to come in between Round Top and Little Round Top, and succeeded in gaining the summit of the latter, when at this time, 6 P. M., Gen. Crawford's division of the Fifth Corps, consisting of two brigades of Pennsylvania Reserves, which until this time had been held back, went into the charge with a terrific shout, driving the Confederates down the rocky front of that hill into the woods, forcing the whole column to retire.

Thus our left was saved and the fight on that part of our lines ended favorably for the day. Our line had, it is true, receded about a third of a mile from that of the morning, but the enemy had been foiled, and we held that natural fortress, Little Round Top. The front of this was immediately covered with a network of breastworks, upon the summit of which were placed twelve thirty-pound Parrott guns. The Pennsylvania Reserve, one company of which was from Gettysburg, fought in sight of their homes, and held this stronghold until the termination of the battle. The fighting ended at this point

CHRISTOPHER SCHMITT,
Lieutenant Battery I, First New York Light Artillery.

THE NEW YORK
PUBLIC LIBRARY

ASTOR, LENOX AND
TILDEN FOUNDATIONS

at 6.30 P. M., but scarcely had it ended on the left but it was renewed on the right. Previous to that time there had been some sharp fighting on this part of the line, but it had ceased. Gen. Ewell, who, it is said, had sworn that he would take and hold at all hazards the hills east of the Baltimore turnpike, on which our right was resting, began to mass his men in that vicinity. Rodes' division was hurried forward from the west end of the town and united with Early's and Johnson's and at 7 P. M. Ewell was ready for action.

During the assault upon Round Top and Little Round Top, Gen. Meade called upon Gen. Newton to weaken the force on Cemetery Hill, in order to assist Gen. Humphreys upon the line of the Emmitsburg road. Accordingly, with others, Lieut. Christopher Schmitt of Wiedrich's Battery with two guns was stationed on the opposite side of the road leading to Taneytown and facing Seminary Ridge within the inclosure of the old cemetery, where he with his two guns assisted during the assault upon Little Round Top, and also took part in that historic artillery duel, resulting in the defeat of the celebrated charge of Pickett's division. Lieut. Schmitt remained at this position during the remainder of the three days' contest.

Gen. Ewell (Confederate) had directed a similar attack to be made at the same hour against the Twelfth Corps in the rear of Culp's Hill, through a valley leading up from Rock Creek toward Spangler's Spring. They may have anticipated an easy conquest here, but two divisions of the Twelfth Corps formed the right flank, west of the creek, and the Second under Gen. Geary occupied Culp's Hill. Only one brigade, the Second, under Gen. Green, remained of Geary's division, the other two, the First and Third, not having returned from the conflict on our left.

Under the cover of the forest and darkness, the enemy confidently advanced as to the accomplishment of an easy task, but they were sadly mistaken. With a desperate courage Green's brigade received them, literally covering the slope of the hill, in front of our works, with the wounded and dead, and the scarred timber in the vicinity attested the obstinacy and effectiveness with which our men fought. In comparison, the enemy's loss was eight to one of ours. Never did men fight with greater determination. From 7 to 9.30 P. M. the roar of musketry was so continuous as to make the very earth tremble. With some minor attacks, this virtually ended Thursday's fight, with decided advantage to the Union Army.

On the part of the enemy, there was some readjusting of their lines during the night. Pickett's division, which had arrived during the evening, was placed to the left of Anderson, and directly opposite our left center; Rodes moving his division to join Ewell's Corps on our right, in order to be ready by dawn to improve the temporary advantage gained the evening before and attempt to obtain possession of Culp's Hill and the Baltimore road. Ewell thus designed to throw his whole force upon our right and break it. This was apparently the programme for our right, while Longstreet was to perform a similar work on our left center.

We now come to the third and last day of this fight, which, for carnage and stubborn resistance, has rarely been equaled. It virtually blocked the attempt of the enemy to invade the States further to the north, as undoubtedly it was their intention originally. On the evening previous a portion of the Twelfth Corps, which had been sent to the left to support Sickles at Little Round Top, returned to the right, and Shaler's brigade of the third division of the Sixth Corps was transferred to the same vicinity, as was also Lockwood's Maryland brigade. Such was our preparation on our part to resist the expected attack.

At dawn our artillery opened upon the enemy at the point where they had made an attack and penetrated our lines, and at sunrise was followed by a general infantry attack, which was maintained with desperate obstinacy on both sides. At eight o'clock a short cessation was had, after which it was renewed with greater earnestness. From 4.30 to 10.30 A. M., with terrible slaughter, the enemy was repulsed and driven over our breastwork with great effect and entirely broken to pieces. A battery placed on a commanding height threw shell over into the enemy's camp. This cannonading lasted for an hour and a half. At 10.30 A. M. the fighting had nearly ceased upon our right, after which it was not renewed on that part of the line. From 11 A. M. to 1 P. M. there was a lull, each party apparently waiting to see what the other was about to do and at what point the attack might be made.

At last this portentous silence was broken. Probably not less than 150 guns on each side sent forth missiles of death, and producing such a succession of thundering sounds, such as perhaps were hardly equaled by the most terrific thunderstorm ever witnessed by mortals. The air was filled by continuous lines of whizzing shells and solid shot. The enemy had placed his guns on the hills near the Bonaughtown road, near the York road, the Harrisburg road, and upon the Seminary Ridge, and along its whole line to a point opposite and south of Round Top, subjecting our artillery on Cemetery Hill to a circle of cross-fires, in order to dismount and destroy them, and by this means to break our front center.

Gen. Lee, having reconnoitered our position, had arrived at the conclusion that our left center was the weakest of our lines —Anderson and McLaw's division having failed to turn our left flank the previous evening. Ewell had also failed to capture Culp's Hill and cemetery, and to turn our right, and now some other point must be assailed, and he concluded to try the point held by Hancock.

At 2.30 P. M. the enemy made a most determined effort to accomplish this result so important to their interests. At this time Pickett's division of Longstreet's Corps, consisting of the brigades of Garnett, Kemper, and Armistead, was seen to emerge from the wooded crest of Seminary Ridge, to the south of McMillan's orchard, and to move in two long and massive lines over the plain toward our left center. This division was supported on the left by Pettigrew's brigade of Heath's division, and on the right by Wright's and Wilcox's brigades of Anderson's division. When this mass of men had moved over about one-third of the space between the two opposing lines, our batteries, which were placed in a grove near Bryan's house, opened upon them, and threw shells and grape into the advancing column; for a few moments they seemed to hesitate; then with a terrific yell they rushed forward. In a moment a tremendous roar, produced from a simultaneous discharge of thousands of muskets, shook the earth; then, in that portion of the line nearest us, a few, then more, and again still more of the enemy, in all not exceeding 200, were perceived moving back toward the point from which they lately had so defiantly proceeded—and at last several men supporting a battle-flag followed the fugitives. The wounded and dead were strewn thickly among the grain and upon the earth, whilst a few men could be seen bearing away upon stretchers a comrade or some favorite commander.

The few officers who survived, for a moment contemplated the scene with amazement, then suddenly and rapidly made their way back to the shelter of the Seminary Ridge. The rank and file of the enemy had been made to believe that they were making a charge upon the Pennsylvania militia, but their belief in this matter was rudely shaken by their first repulse, but still they pressed on. Gen. Gibbon had ordered the infantry to fall back, so as to enable the artillery to use grape. On they came to the cannon's mouth and at the first discharge were blown or cut down by hundreds. Seeing the enemy waver, Gen. Wells cried out, " Boys, the enemy is ours," and, rushing upon them with his brigade, captured 800 prisoners. Stannard's brigade took as many more, and others completed the task, swelling the number of prisoners to 3,500. Fifteen stands of colors were taken, and so sudden and complete was the slaughter and capture of Pickett's men, that it is said that one of the officers who fell wounded in the first charge, and who characterized it as a mad and foolish scheme, said that when, in a few moments afterwards, he was enabled to rise and look about him, the whole division had disappeared as if blown away by the wind. In this mad charge of the enemy Gens. Kemper and Armistead were wounded and Garnett killed. Of our force Gens. Hancock and Gibbon were wounded.

While this was happening at this point the enemy was not inactive on his extreme right, and showed considerable vigor opposite Little Round Top. Hood's division was repulsed in attempting to drive our force from that stronghold. To complete our victory upon the line the Pennsylvania Reserves were called upon to make a charge upon a battery just in front of them. The Reserves took the battery, 300 prisoners, and 5,000 stand of arms, and drove them half a mile beyond the line they had occupied during the day.

This virtually ended the Battle of Gettysburg, which has been given in some detail to enable the reader to understand its general features and the stubborn resistance shown by our brave men, of which our own city furnished many. From this Battery three of its members were killed and ten wounded, which, notwithstanding the desperate fighting, was more than the average of the losses sustained by the other batteries from this State in that action; and, to sum up, the total loss of the New York State troops was:

	Officers.	Men.
Killed	77	838
Wounded	298	3,737
Missing	69	1,708
A total loss of		6,777

We conclude Gettysburg with an extract from the report of the commission: "By common consent this famous battle-field has been chosen to signalize the patriotism, valor and fortitude of the defenders of the Union in the great Civil War of 1861–65. It was a decisive victory, won at a moment when defeat might have been ruinous to our cause. The assaults upon our lines at Gettysburg were made by the most powerful army ever encountered by the Union forces, and 307 commands in the Army of the Potomac officially report losses at Gettysburg amounting in the aggregate to 22,990 officers and men, and of these the eighty-seven New York commands in this battle lost 6,777, nearly one-third of the total number of casualties." The defeat, therefore, of Gen. Lee and the Southern forces upon this field was the beginning of the end culminating at Appomattox.

Some extracts, only, from a very full report of Gen. O. O. Howard of his command during the battle of Gettysburg are given as follows:

. . . . And that Gen. Hancock should further arrange the disposition of the troops, while I should take the right of the same, and in a very short time we put the troops in position, as I had previously directed, excepting that Gen. Wadsworth's division was sent to occupy a height to the right and rear of our position. In passing through the town we lost many prisoners, but the enemy, perceiving the strength of our position on the height, made no further attempt to renew the engagement that evening.

About 7 P. M. (July 1st) Gens. Slocum and Sickles arrived at the cemetery. A formal order was at the same time put into my hands, placing Gen. Hancock in command of the left wing. But Gen. Slocum being present, and senior, I turned my command over to him and resumed the direct command of the Eleventh Corps; whereupon Gen. Hancock repaired to the headquarters of Gen. Meade.

The eventful day was over. The First and Eleventh Corps, numbering less than 18,000 men, notably aided by Buford's division of cavalry, had engaged and held in check nearly double their numbers from ten o'clock in the morning until seven in the evening. They gave way, it is true, after hard fighting, yet they secured and held the remarkable position which, under the able generalship of the commander of this army, contributed to the grand results of July 2d and 3d.

This day's battle cost us many valuable lives. Major-Gen. Reynolds, a noble commander and long a personal friend, fell early in the action. Lieut. Bayard Wilkeson,* a young officer of exceeding promise, was mortally wounded while in command of Battery G, Fourth United States Artillery. Brigadier-Generals Barlow and Paul were severely wounded. For mention of other distinguished officers killed and wounded, I would refer you to reports of corps, division and brigade commanders.

Major Osborn, commanding artillery of Eleventh Corps, reports that his artillery dismounted five of the enemy's guns, which were left on the field.

*　　*　　*　　*　　*　　*　　*

On the morning of July 2d, about 3 A. M., the commanding general, who had previously arrived, met me at the cemetery gate, questioned me about the preceding day and rode with me over the position then held by our troops. I expressed my opinion strongly in favor of the position. The general replied that he was glad to hear me speak thus, for it was too late to leave it.

The Eleventh Corps was disposed with its center near the Baltimore pike; the first division, Gen. Ames, on the right; third division, Gen. Schurz, in the center, and the second division, Gen.

* Lieut. Wilkeson was a nephew of Mr. John Wilkeson of this city.

Steinwehr, on the left. The batteries of the First and Eleventh Corps were united, being put in position with regard to the kind of gun. Col. Wainwright, chief of artillery First Corps, took charge of all batteries to the right of the pike; Major Osborn, of the Eleventh, of all batteries in the cemetery grounds to the left of the pike. Very little occurred while the other corps were coming into position until about 4 P. M. Just before this, orders had been issued to the division commanders to make ready for battle, as the enemy were reported advancing on our left. Now the enemy opened from some dozen batteries on our right and front, bringing a concentrated fire upon our position. The batteries of Wainwright and Osborn replied with great spirit. Artillery projectiles often struck among the men, but in no case did a regiment break, though suffering considerably.

About 6.30 P. M. I sent word to Gen. Meade that the enemy's batteries on our extreme right had been silenced or withdrawn. After the cannonading had ceased, and the enemy's infantry attack upon the left had been repulsed, another attack, said to be by Rodes' division, commenced between 7 and 8 P. M., beginning between Gens. Slocum and Wadsworth, and extending along in front of Ames to the town of Gettysburg. A brigade of Gen. Schurz's division was ordered to support Gen. Ames. Another brigade of Gen. Schurz pushed to the support of Gen. Wadsworth upon his right. Afterwards Gen. Greene, of the Twelfth Corps, came to thank me for the good service done by this brigade. . . . .

The attack was so sudden and violent that the infantry in front of Ames was giving way. In fact, at one moment the enemy had got within the batteries. A request for assistance had already gone to headquarters, so that promptly a brigade of the Second Corps, under Col. Carroll, moved to Ames' right, deployed and went into position just in time to check the enemy's advance. At Wiedrich's Battery, Gen. Ames by extraordinary exertions arrested a panic, and the men with sponge-staffs and bayonets forced the enemy back. At this time he received support from Gen. Schurz. Effective assistance was also rendered at this time by a portion of Gen. Steinwehr's command, at points where the enemy was breaking through. This furious onset was met and withstood at every point, and lasted less than an hour.

From the report of Maj.-Gen. Carl Schurz, commanding Third Division, to Maj.-Gen. Howard, commanding Eleventh Corps:

. . . . At nine o'clock the enemy was repulsed at that point, and no further demonstration made. While this was going on, between 8 and 9 P. M., we suddenly heard a rapid musketry fire on eminence immediately east of the cemetery, where Captain Wiedrich's Battery stood. You ordered me to take two regiments across the road to the aid of that battery. This order was executed by two regiments of the second brigade, the One Hundred and Nineteenth, and Fifty-eighth New York, headed by Col. Krzyranowski, commanding second brigade. I at once hastened with my whole staff toward the threatened point, driving back stragglers with our swords as we went. To my great surprise, we found a general *mêlée* in the battery itself, the enemy's infantry having already gotten possession of some of the guns. The cannoneers were defending themselves valiantly. Our infantry made a vigorous rush upon the intruders, and, after a short and very spirited hand-to-hand fight, succeeded in driving them down the hill. I cannot refrain from speaking of the conduct of the officers and men on that occasion with the greatest satisfaction.

From the report of Emil Koenig, Captain, commanding 58th Regiment, New York Volunteers:

. . . . About 4 P. M. (on July 2d), the rebels opened a murderous fire upon our division from three or four batteries in different positions, which was briskly responded to by the batteries of Captains Wiedrich and Dilcher, on the right and left of the division. . . . . During all this time my men exhibited great courage and coolness. About 8 P. M. our regiment was ordered ahead, and to the left of the brigade, behind a stone fence, where we were exposed to a severe artillery fire, which, however, did us no damage. Suddenly we were ordered to the right, where a column of the enemy, coming up under cover of the darkness, had tried to storm Captain Wiedrich's Battery, but was repulsed before we arrived. . . . . At six o'clock in the morning we were ordered to the right of the road leading to Gettysburg. We were posted behind a stone fence to the left of Captain Wiedrich's Battery.

An omission to report by its commanding officer, a captain, for some unexplained reason, has had the effect of throwing out on paper, during the assault of the "Tigers," July 2d, the 73d Pennsylvania Regiment, which was a part of the second division, first brigade, under Col. Coster—which brigade was composed of the 134th New York Volunteers, the 154th New York Volunteers, the 27th and 73d Pennsylvania Volunteers. In the several reports of that day, I cannot find any mention made of the 73d Pennsylvania, although attached as above.

This regiment, I am assured by Col. Wiedrich, was on his left and assisted in this repulse—honor to whom honor is due. The 73d have erected upon these heights their monument, which would not have been allowed if not deserved.

Gen. Steinwehr, says: "I placed the first brigade, Colonel Charles R. Coster, on the northeast end of the hill, in support of Wiedrich's Battery, which was there in position."

The 27th Pennsylvania Volunteers are specially mentioned. Here follows the casualties of that regiment, and also of the 73d Pennsylvania, which may prove that the latter also *saw service* at Gettysburg:

27th Pennsylvania—killed, 2 officers, 4 men; wounded, 3 officers, 26 men; missing, 1 officer, 75 men; total, 111.

73d Pennsylvania—killed, 7 men; wounded, 27 men; total, 34.

Deducting the 75 missing men of the 27th Pennsylvania, there is only a difference in their favor of two men lost.

Extract from a fragment of a diary, without date or signature, now in Col. Wiedrich's possession:

July 1, 2 and 3, Gettysburg.—On arriving near Gettysburg, Pa., about 11 A. M., July 1, we were ordered to a position on Cemetery Hill, north of the Baltimore turnpike, which position we held until the close of the battle, on the evening of July 3d. During the three days' fighting we had three men killed, two officers and nine men wounded. The dead were buried in the Cemetery of Gettysburg, and the wounded sent to Baltimore, Md.

Extract of a letter to the New York *Times*, written by Mr. L. L. Crounse, its correspondent:

. . . . The formation of the ground on the right and center was excellent for defensive purposes. On our extreme left the ground sloped off until the position was no higher than the enemy's. The ground in front of our line was a level, open country, interspersed here and there with an orchard or a very fine tract of trees, generally oak. . . . .

Gen. Howard occupied with his corps a beautiful cemetery on a hill to the south of Gettysburg. Cannons thundered, horses pranced, and men carelessly trampled over the ruins of the dead. . . . From this hill a beautiful view could be obtained of the valley, and also of goodly portions of the enemy's line of battle. . . . . A great and manifest feature of this battle is the splendid use of artillery.

CASUALTIES OF THIS BATTERY AT GETTYSBURG.

Killed — Jacob Kimmel, Mathias Kussenberger and Edward Sonnenborg.

Wounded—Lieut. Nicholas Sahm, Lieut. Christian Stock, William Hartmann, Albert Brauner, Philip Mathis, Jacob Weller, Jacob Willig, John Kappel and Andrew Zimmer.

Under date of September 30th, it is stated that letters have been received announcing that Wiedrich's Battery has been ordered to join Gen. Rosecrans at Chattanooga, "as it has proved to be one of the most serviceable artillery organizations of the Army of the Potomac, and will, if an opportunity offers, gain fresh laurels at the West."

From a dispatch dated Chicago, October 5th, it states that the 11th and 12th Army Corps, Gens. Howard and Slocum, were passing through that city for three days, and destined for Nashville, Tenn, but the Battery, with a portion of the Eleventh Corps, to which it belonged, went by way of Indianapolis. Later, in speaking of the enemy: "It is supposed they will concentrate their artillery at Missionary Ridge; many of their pieces are heavy and all seem to carry well. They hold both Lookout Mountain and Missionary Ridge. We have several lines of intrenchments and extensive earthworks. The plan of the enemy appears not to make an attack in the front, but compel us to abandon Chattanooga, by simply holding us in our present position, with their army in our front, annoying us with their artillery and by breaking our lines of connection, by cavalry raids in our rear."

While at Chattanooga, a pleasant incident occurs in which is shown, that while one may be deeply afflicted, yet, truly sympathetic, loses no opportunity of attempting to lift the cloud of sorrow from others.

Mr. James E. Murdock, whose son was killed upon the field of Chickamauga, was at this place for the purpose of obtaining the body, and while awaiting the movements of the officials in the matter, deemed it his duty to administer to the comfort of those in the hospitals. He spent, therefore, much of his time reading to the sick and giving entertainments to the able-bodied ones. These kindly acts were fully appreciated by the veterans.

February 10, 1864: "We learn that Captain Wiedrich has been promoted to the Lieutenant-Colonelcy of the 15th New York Heavy Artillery. The Colonel if he has not sought the bubble reputation, has earned the 'Eagles,' even in the cannon's mouth, and none more worthy to wear them than he."

February 16th, we find "that Captain Wiedrich is at home with Lieut. Sahm, and sixty-four of his gallant men, all of whom have re-enlisted. They arrived Saturday night from Bridgeport, Alabama. As a majority of the Battery have re-enlisted, enough to place it on a maximum footing, probably a recruiting office will not be opened."

On Monday, the 14th of March, a number of the friends of Captain Wiedrich assembled at Gillig's Hall, and presented the Battery a beautiful silk flag, made by the lady friends of the Battery, and was presented in a fitting speech by Police Commissioner Jacob Beyer, and responded to by Captain Wiedrich. The flag is now in the custody of the State of New York, at Albany. An attempt was made at the time of the dedication of the monument at Gettysburg to obtain it for that occasion, but refused by the Adjutant-General. A duplicate was made and used.

THE BATTLES NEAR CHATTANOOGA.

A description of the scenes and incidents of this campaign would be incomplete, probably unsatisfactory, without a brief sketch of the locality, and a sufficient outline to assist the comprehension of movements which led up to the situation of armies and the culminating battles of November, 1863.

Protestant missionaries were here laboring among the Creek and Cherokee tribes in 1817, the Rev. Cyrus Kingsbury being the pioneer. He was shortly joined by co-workers, and missionary stations Brainard and Elliott were established.

The name Mission Mills needs no interpretation. The origin of Missionary Ridge is equally plain.

Soldiers of the Union Army abbreviate the name to Mission, ex-Confederates refer to it as Missionary Ridge. The name Chattanooga is derived from two Indian words, *Chatta*, place of, *Ooga*, rocks. It is now many years since the Government decree to remove the Indians from this vicinity was enforced. How, may be inferred from the statement subsequently made, that more than five thousand aged persons and children perished by the way. Those Indians who clung to their old homes were forced out by the soldiers, and whites who defended them were punished by law for their crime.* It is said that John Howard Payne was among those who suffered. Chattanooga, then Ross Landing, grew from a settlement to a village. In 1861 it was a town of considerable population, evidencing enterprise, and a point towards which the attention of commanding officers of both the Union and Confederate armies was early directed. The vicinity of Chattanooga was reached by Union troops but no occupation was effected until September, 1863, when Gen. Rosecrans skillfuly manœuvred Gen. Bragg's forces out of the town and immediate vicinity.

After referring to the difficulties of transportation which beset the accumulation of ammunition sufficient for advance, plans for which Gen. Rosecrans had already matured, Gen. Boynton mentions with some comment Gen. Halleck's imperative orders telegraphed persistently from Washington.

Gen. Rosecrans pushed his preparations, and as he could not obtain forage for the animals, or transport it in quantities, he waited till the corn had ripened, and when it had, having in the meantime accumulated twenty-five days' rations and a liberal supply of ammunition, he gave orders for the advance.

By a brilliant feint, extending through the mountains north of Chattanooga toward Buckner's forces in East Tennessee, the appearance of four brigades opposite the city, on the line from Kingston above to the mouth of Lookout Valley below, and of a division in the Sequatchie Valley east of the first range of the Cumberlands, he had wholly deceived Bragg as to the movement, and the entire army effected a crossing in the vicinity of Bridgeport without special opposition.

* The compiler of this work feels a personal interest in this locality; also the subsequent place in Mississippi to where those Indians were removed, as his parents were, in 1821, appointed to the Mission under the Rev. Cyrus Kingsbury, of whom he also is a namesake.

The facts of the crossing show that Rosecrans had moved at the earliest possible moment. He did not even take time to bring up sufficient bridges. Brannan's division crossed at the mouth of Battle Creek on rafts and in canoes which the men cut out for themselves. In fact, those who could swim well did not wait either for rafts or canoes, but put their guns and clothing on a few fence rails and pushed these before them over the wide stream. The artillery was ferried on a single pontoon, which would not carry a piece and its limber at the same time. Another division was taken over at Bridgeport in small boats. The crossings began on the 28th of August, the river being, at the points selected, 1,200 feet at the narrowest and 2,700 feet at the widest point. In spite of the very limited bridge facilities for any portion of the troops, and the fact that some divisions were without any, at the end of seven days the army was on the south bank, ready for its mountain marches.

Once across, the columns moved with expedition. They had before them, and between them and the valleys that led from the south into Chattanooga, the precipitous Sand Mountains and Lookout ranges. These were of the general height of the Cumberland Mountains, very steep, with rock palisades along the summits. The trails which crossed them were narrow and exceedingly difficult for teams, in fact impassable for loaded trains, except where, as in any army, there is unlimited command of horse and man power. The teams were doubled both for baggage wagons and artillery, and, in addition, at the steepest points, ropes at which entire companies pulled were also attached. An idea of the difficulties of ascending these mountains will be gained by a knowledge of the fact that it required from sundown to sunrise for the artillery and moderate train of a single brigade, thus assisted, to reach the summit of the first range. But by utilizing every trail, and working day and night, at the end of the fourth day, namely, September 8, the whole army had crossed Sand Mountains and descended into Lookout Valley, and the heads of its columns had gained the summit of Lookout at two points, one 25 and the other 42 miles south of the river, from which positions they looked down upon Bragg's communications. Crittenden's corps had moved down the valley toward the north point of Lookout, where it occupied the position of an observing force near Chattanooga.

When Gen. Bragg found the Union Army on the south bank of the river threatening his supplies, he evacuated Chattanooga, withdrawing to Lafayette, 25 miles southeast, to await reinforcements from Mississippi, and the arrival of Longstreet from Virginia.

On the 9th of September, Crittenden's division passed around the point of the mountain into Chattanooga. It was this appearance of one division in the city which gave rise to the report, still generally believed, that the Army of the Cumberland had occupied Chattanooga without a battle, had moved thence to attack Bragg, had been overwhelmed at Chickamauga, and driven back again in confused and disastrous retreat to Chattanooga. But Crittenden only left a brigade in the city, and passed through, following Bragg's retreat for purposes of observation and to join the rest of the army then emerging from the passes over Lookout into the valley far south of Chattanooga.

The probable reasons why General Rosecrans did not concentrate his army about Chattanooga, are given at length by General Boynton, the principal being that the position of his corps was unfavorable to such a movement in the face of so wary a foe as General Bragg, and misleading information as to reinforcements.

The Battle of Chickamauga occurred on the 19th and 20th of September, ten days subsequent. The conflict to the last was desperate, as the following will show.

THE LAST ASSAULT AT CHICKAMAUGA.

"Longstreet's last assault began shortly before five o'clock and lasted two hours. In preparing for it he asked Bragg for reinforcements from the right, but was informed, as Longstreet reports, 'that they had been beaten back so badly that they could be of no service to me.' Preston's fine division of four brigades, which up to that hour had not been in the battle, were given the advance. Behind this line were Kershaw's troops, and Johnston's and Hindman's and Stewart's divisions. All these, with yells and a mighty momentum, once more rushed up the slopes of the range. An army was assaulting three thin divisions. There were ten Confederate brigades in front of the four which Brannan and Granger had in line, and four of these in Longstreet's column were veterans who had not fired a gun in the battle. The assaulting force before Wood was about in the same proportion. But Granger, Brannan and Wood stood immovable. To those present on either side, the memory of those hours is of the severest musketry of their experience. It never slackened, except as ammunition ran low at times on the Union side, and in place of firing came the cheers of the charging lines as they rushed down with the bayonet upon the ascending column. Hindman, from the Army of Northern Virginia, declared he had never seen Union soldiers fight as well, and never saw Confederate troops fight better. Seen from the base of the range, its summit was sheeted with fire and smoke, or gleamed with its hedge of steel. Pressing up its slopes, line followed line from below, and from above came line after line torn, bleeding, dying, tumbling over on those behind, while on the crest the contracting Union lines closed over their wounded and their dead, and stood unmoved in their places under the flag till the sun went down and the road for which they had contended was won.

"Just before dusk Steedman was withdrawn from Brannan's right, leaving Vanderveer's Brigade the right of the army for the closing half hour of the fight, as it had been the left of the line when the battle opened on the first day. And here the 35th Ohio, of this brigade, which the first day received the brunt of the final rebel effort on the left, drove back a line of Longstreet's men, which had gained the ridge when Steedman's withdrew, and fired the last volley of the day. Brannan's division had formerly been General Thomas' own command, and Vanderveer's brigade in Thomas' division as far back as Mill Springs. He well knew both brigade and division, and made of both his flying forces for use on all parts of the line."

No description can convey more than an idea of the steadfast valor and the terrific onsets of that field. Only the strength of defensive position and furious, never-flinching fighting saved Thomas' lines from the magnificent assaults of Bragg's forces. When the sun went down the second day 30,000 killed and wounded attested the courage, the devotion and effective fighting of those engaged. The campaign was a success for Rosecrans. The battle was the full revelation of Thomas—the most perfect military character of Union history—and the matchless fighting along his lines glorified the private soldiers who held them steady and saved an army.

General Cist states, "that General Rosecrans had on the field 55,000 effective men, opposed to Bragg's 70,000 troops in line, and that Rosecrans' losses aggregated 1,687 killed, 9,394 wounded, 5,255 missing; total 16,336. Bragg's losses, in part estimated, were 2,673 killed, 16,274 wounded, and 2,003 missing, a total of 20,950. A full report of rebel losses was never made."

Chattanooga was converted into a fortress, the outer lines of which extended from the bluffs on the river above to the bank of the river below the town, which was encircled and covered from all land approach. These works, a little more than three miles in extent, were strengthened wherever possible, by special fortifications. Forts Wood and Negley, Batteries Sheridan, Rosseau, Cheatham, were among these within this line. Other works were built, all finally covered by the fort on Cameron Hill. To an assault, Chattanooga was practically impregnable. The question of forage and rations was the problem to be solved. General Bragg with his army occupied Missionary Ridge, from which to Lookout Mountain a strong line of rifle-pits crossed Chattanooga Valley. Lookout, a fortress in itself, had been strengthened by rifle-pits. The only possible route for supplies was forty miles long, across mountain ranges, over roads which were such in name alone. Day by day the starved battery horses fell dead at the picket ropes, and rigid economy of food was everywhere practiced. Matters grew more and more desperate. The road over Waldron's Ridge was fringed with dead mules. Soldiers had unsoldered their canteens, and with nails improvised graters, with which to provide meal when ears of corn could be obtained. The bark of young cottonwood trees sustained such mules as had perforce acquired an inclination for it. These were starvation times in Chattanooga, and, to add to the hardship, the weather was unusually severe for that region, and fuel difficult to obtain.

With the situation as outlined, it would seem impossible that the morale of the army should be what it was. The troops were cheerful, and confident as to the future. The relief of General Rosecrans occasioned unquestionable regret, but the confidence of the army in General Thomas was unbounded.

The transportation of General Hooker with the Eleventh and Twelfth Corps from the Army of the Potomac to Bridgeport, was under the personal supervision of Col. Thomas A. Scott, with such lieutenants as Frank Thomson as aids. General Grant reached Chattanooga on the night of October 23d.

Plans already in progress to open and control the navigation of the Tennessee River were examined and ordered executed under the supervision of General W. F. Smith, Chief Engineer of the Army of the Cumberland. Under cover of darkness fifteen hundred gallant men of Hazen's brigade floated from Chattanooga down the Tennessee to Brown's Ferry.

The enemy's pickets and batteries were passed without discovery, and at dawn on October 27th the lodgment at Brown's Ferry was complete, being held by Hazen's and Turching's brigades, protected by ample fortifications. The same afternoon Hooker's advance occupied Wauhatchie in Lookout Valley, and at night repelled a vigorous attack made by Longstreet's men who were driven back to their camps at Lookout, after a short but determined engagement. Hooker's occupation of Lookout Valley settled the question of supplies, and Chattanooga was presently filled with the stores of food and ammunition. Heavy ordnance replaced field batteries in the fortifications, and much needed clothing was provided for the soldiers.

For the safety of Burnside's position at Knoxville there was apprehension which became grave from the fact that Longstreet's command, reinforced by troops from Bragg's immediate army, was marching toward East Tennessee. But Sherman was close at hand. After a march of 400 miles, his leading division reached Brown's Ferry, November 18th.

Two of his divisions crossed and moved along concealed roads, through the woods and behind the hills to a point on the north bank of the river eight miles above the town, near the mouth of the North Chickamauga and opposite Bragg's position on the northern extremity of Missionary Ridge. Here they were camped out of sight. The breaking of the bridge at Brown's Ferry prevented the crossing of the third division. On the 22d of November the Eleventh Corps, under Howard, composed of Schurz's and Steinwehr's divisions, was brought over the bridge from Hooker's position, marched into the town, and given prominent position in the line, to convey the impression to the enemy watching from the heights that the town was being reinforced by the troops passing on the bridge, and thus direct attention from Sherman's movements, and the preparations for the crossing at the North Chickamauga.

The first contest opened on the Union side with what the enemy mistook for a grand review, but which suddenly and unexpectedly developed into a battle worthy of the initial move in the series to follow. In front of Fort Wood and its adjacent batteries, located in the eastern limits of the city, and looking out over the plain towards Missionary Ridge, the ground at first descends rapidly, and then rolls gently away, furnishing abundant space for a great review. About noon of November 23d, this portion of the plain and the open country to the right and left of it began, under orders from General Thomas, to fill with troops. First Wood's division moved out and deployed. Sheridan followed and took position farther to the right and slightly to the rear. Howard's Corps, massed by divisions and brigades, marched with the precision of a review into place in rear of Wood and Sheridan. Baird moved out of the works to the right of the latter, and formed in echelon in his rear, while Johnston's division stood to arms in the intrenchments in rear of the center. For a brief time, while the various commanders were receiving their orders, this grand pageant of twenty thousand men, ready for a spring on the enemy's advanced line, stood motionless as if for review. The rebel pickets leaned lazily on their guns, enjoying the spectacle. Groups of Confederates could be seen on Lookout, on Orchard Knob, and along the ridge, watching the display. Even the forward movement of the leading deployed divisions did not dispel the illusion until the Union picket-line advanced, firing. Wood, followed by an army on his flanks and in rear, moved rapidly on Orchard Knob, a mile and a quarter to the front, sweeping away pickets and reserves, and carrying the Knob and hill on the right. Sheridan swiftly moved upon and grasped the positions still farther to the right. Howard's two divisions deployed to the left, and after sharp fighting occupied the rebel line in his front. Before night the vast drill ground, over which an army under guise of a review had moved to the attack with the precision of parade, had been extended until the entire advanced line of the enemy, two miles in length, was in the possession of these very practical columns of review. Seldom had troops moved under more inspiring circumstances. On the Union side, Grant and Thomas, with crowds of staff officers, the population of a city, and thousands of their comrades, looked down upon them from the town. From the enemy's line a large part of the Confederate army on its many heights was watching them. The heavy guns from the forts covering the movement called universal attention to their imposing advance and gave the added inspiration of a tremendous cannonade. Thus incited, the quiet but magnificent pageant developed into the swift advance and speedy victory of an army. The captured line afforded distinct views of the rebel works along the foot of the Ridge beyond, and the exact character of the ground before them, and formed an excellent base for the final assault which two days later closed the battle and gave victory to the Union arms.

While this movement was in progress Sherman was laboring hard to concentrate his forces for crossing the river, but the bridge at the ferry breaking again, while one of his divisions was still on the south bank, the plan of battle was changed for the second time, and Hooker was ordered to move at daylight and attack Lookout. For this he had Geary's division of the Twelfth Corps, the delayed division of Sherman's column, under Osterhaus, and two brigades of Cruft's division or the Fourth Corps; troops which thus first met each other while advancing in actual battle.

It was a busy night on both sides. Believing that an assault on Lookout was the least likely of all, and that the next blow would fall on his right, Bragg during the night withdrew an entire division from the mountain to strengthen the Ridge. All night long the rebel signal torches were waving in the sight of both armies from all the heights, busily writing their mysterious characters of fire against the sky. Hooker, in Lookout Valley, was preparing his forces to move at daylight, against the craggy heights above him. At midnight, far away on the other flank, one hundred and sixteen boats, carrying General Giles A. Smith's brigade of Sherman's men floated silently out of the mouth of North Chickamauga, and shot rapidly to the south bank of the Tennessee. The enemy's pickets were surprised, and a landing made near the mouth of South Chickamauga Creek without serious opposition. At daylight two divisions were over, a strong bridge-head had been constructed, the bridge itself was well advanced, and Sherman's forces stood facing the strongly fortified right flank of the Confederate position. Wood and Sheridan used the night for strengthening their lines, and placing batteries on the hills they had captured. As the light grew strong enough to reveal positions, the enemy's attention was mainly fixed on Sherman's threatening position. Bragg's expectation of an attact on his right seemed about to be realized, as three divisions moved forward and slowly deployed a little more than a mile away. But the real mysteries of this second day were veiled by the fogs on Lookout. Under the impenetrable curtain Hooker was arranging his lines for an assault which a few hours later was to present to the hosts of both armies, on the plains and lesser ridges below, a drama of battle played on such lofty summits, and so wrapped in cloud-effects of fog, as to seem more like a contest raging in the skies than one borne upward on the solid mountain.

A brief preliminary sketch of the position, somewhat more in detail than the general view already presented, is needed to fix the features of the wonderful scene in mind. Advancing toward Chattanooga from the south, along the crest of Lookout Mountain, the road traverses a gently broken table-land of very considerable width, terminated on each side by high precipices. For two miles before reaching the point of the mountain, which looks down upon the city and is fourteen hundred feet above it, this table-land narrows to a width of half a mile, and the precipices on either side are about one hundred feet in height. From the base of those sheer rocky walls the mountain slopes on the right to Chattanooga Creek, on the left to Lookout Creek, and directly under the point downward to the Tennessee. These slopes of the mountain are something over a mile in extent, and the streams, both in the eastern and the western valley, require bridges. Except on the portions facing the town, which had been partially cleared for farming, the ground was everywhere crossed with ledges of rock, strewn with detached masses from the precipices above, tangled with fallen timber, and studded with sufficient forest to conceal defensive works and forces. The only road to the summit led up from Chattanooga Valley from a point within the Confederate lines. These apparently impracticable slopes had been heavily fortified against approach from Hooker's position, and, after the withdrawal the night before of one division, were still held by six brigades, which, counting the immense strength of position and works, almost equaled as many divisions for offensive purposes.

At eight o'clock in the morning of the 24th, Geary crossed Lookout Creek, about two miles up the valley, with his own division and Whittaker's brigade of the Fourth Corps, and under cover of the fog marched directly up the western slope of the mountain till his right rested at the foot of the palisades, his left reaching the base of the mountain below. Meantime a brigade had forced the passage of the creek half a mile above the rebel intrenchments, and planted artillery to enfilade one portion of their line. Guns had also been dragged to the tops of several high hills in the valley, while batteries were brought close to the enemy's lines at a bridge near the mouth of the creek, where the division of Osterhaus confronted the rebel works. A section of twenty-pounder Parrotts was hauled to an elevation that would enable them to reach the camps on the upper slopes, and the heavy casemated guns of Brannan, on Moccasin Point, across the river, were made ready to open on the front of the mountain.

All these preparations to strike had progressed under cover of the night and the morning fog, and had only provoked brisk picket-firing, which was inaudible in the main Union lines. While the sounds of general movement rose through the fog, its character could not be ascertained by the enemy above till the blows began to fall; and the distance to Bragg's headquarters on Missionary Ridge and the impossibility of signaling prevented any notification of the great stir in Lookout Valley reaching him, and so he continued to give chief attention to Sherman's demonstration. At eleven o'clock, Geary's line, sweeping the slope from palisades to base, reached the forces posted with the enfilading artillery. Here, while the Union lines were being re-arranged and reinforced for their great swing against the rebel works and around the point of the mountain, nature's vast curtain of fog began to rise upon the opening scenes of the great drama.

Suddenly the Union batteries opened on the mountain, calling the enemy's attention away from Sherman's threatening movements, and announcing unexpected battle around the crags of Lookout. Except where Sherman was advancing, silence fell along the many miles of opposing lines, from every part of which the Confederate works on the front of the mountain could be seen. From the valley beyond these, and so behind the mountain, came the sound of the volleys of Geary's advance. More than a hundred thousand spectators stood motionless, listening intently, with gaze fixed on the points where the storm of battle, roaring down the western valley, might be expected to burst over the front of the mountain. Just before the contending lines came into view the fog lifted still higher, and a scene such as battle-story cannot surpass was clearly revealed. Its appearance was announced by the crashing shot of many guns and the cheers of charging infantry, which drove the Confederates from their lower works and forced them back to their main lines. The Union line could be plainly seen in its advance, its flags dotting the front at intervals, from the precipices above to the river bluff below. The heavy batteries on Moccasin Point continually burst their shells in front of this line; the rebel artillery flamed in its very face, and volley after volley rained on its advancing, but never-halting, veterans. As the sharp contest for the rebel line in the open space went on, the Union forces in the plain below cheered, seemingly as soldiers never could have cheered before, and all the bands along that front of many miles played on and on, while Hooker's lines, ten thousand strong, swept around the mountain, pushing the enemy from its front, and forcing him southward along its eastern slopes.

At two o'clock the heavy fighting was done, and the lower stronghold of the mountain had been wrested from the enemy. Carlin's brigade from Chattanooga marched with supplies of ammunition up the mountain to Hooker's right, under the palisades, and did good service at the close of the day. All night the flash of rifles from the outposts shone through the fog; and when morning broke it had not yet been determined whether the enemy had withdrawn from his unassailable position on the top of the mountain.

The day dawned clear. All eyes in the Union bivouacs were strained towards the summit. Gradually it grew purple with the strengthening light; and just as the sun broke over it a squad of men walked out on the rock overhanging the precipice at the point of the mountain, and, in the view of the watching and breathless thousands, unfurled the Stars and Stripes. Once more cheers and music swept along the plain, and an army of veterans looked long through its tears at this mute announcement of a second victory.

Then came the closing scene and fitting culmination of the three days' pageant. While Hooker's assault on Lookout was at its height, Sherman moved unmolested, and at 4 P. M. had apparently carried the northern extremity of Missionary Ridge. The mystery of this failure to oppose him was explained by the discovery that the elevations he had occupied were not a part of the continuous Ridge, but that Bragg's strongly fortified flank rested on the next hills to the south. At this point the heavy fighting of the closing day began in Sherman's effort to carry the rebel right.

The cheering of the flag displayed on Lookout, at sunrise on the 25th, had scarcely died away before Sherman moved to the attack, and the sounds of action turned universal attention away from the mountain to the Union left. Hooker also moved at daylight through Chattanooga Valley, driving before him the rear-guard of the column retreating from Lookout. On reaching Rossville, after sharp fighting, he ascended Missionary Ridge, and, forming his lines across it, threatened Bragg's left. He had, however, been much delayed by the necessity of bridging Chattanooga Creek, and Sherman on the right had been furiously fighting many hours before Hooker gained position. The entire rebel army was now concentrated upon Missionary Ridge, covering its crest for about six miles. Four divisions of the Army of the Cumberland faced three miles of this position, occupying the works which had been carried in the first day's advance. Howard's Corps of the same army, still farther to the left, confronted the Ridge to a point within a mile of Sherman. During the forenoon Confederate troops could be plainly seen moving along the summit, strengthening their center, and massing heavily against Sherman.

The plan of battle made Sherman's advance the guiding movement. His center was to carry the northern extremity of the Ridge, while his wings swept its western and eastern slopes. The Army of the Cumberland, closing to the left, was to join Sherman's right, and, moving southerly with his line, clear the Valley to the base of the Ridge and aid in the flank attack on the lower line of works.

The battle opened early by three brigades of Sherman's troops descending the hills they had occupied the day before, which had at first been supposed to be a part of the continuous Ridge, and assaulting the works of Bragg's right on the next heights beyond. These rested not only across the

GEORGE F SCHWARTZ,
Lieutenant Battery I, First New York Light Artillery.

THE NEW YORK
PUBLIC LIBRARY

ASTOR, LENOX AND
TILDEN FOUNDATIONS
R   L

Ridge, but extended along lateral spurs, which gave abundant room for strong works, and the operations of a heavy defending force. The moment Sherman's leading brigade moved out of the cover of woods on the hills, and began to descend into the gorge separating them from the enemy, they were exposed to a murderous fire; but after reaching the valley they rushed upward to the attack, and seized and held a spur within a hundred yards of the rebel works. From this point assault followed assault, the Union line being constantly swept back by the concentrated fire of the Confederate lines delivered almost in their faces. Howard's Corps was sent to Sherman from Thomas' left as early as ten o'clock, and six divisions were then engaged in the attempt to capture the extremity of the Ridge. Still, every front assault, though made on all parts of the line with the utmost courage, was hurled back, and the same fate met the flank attacks on the eastern and western slopes.

The terrible pendulum swings of Sherman's troops against the heights—more terrible because seemingly fruitless—were plainly seen from Orchard Knob, where Grant, Thomas and Sheridan stood watching the contest hour after hour, with an intensity of interest and a growing impatience which were inseparable from the situation. The sun was nearing the western ranges, Hooker's guns had not been heard on the right, and Sherman was unable with all his force to make further impression on the left. Baird was hurried to his aid. He then had seven divisions, or over half the Union Army, but there being no room for Baird to operate, he returned to the center, and had just formed again on the left of the Army of the Cumberland, when the grand spectacular movement began which closed the fight.

THE STORMING OF MISSIONARY RIDGE.

It came from a sudden change in the plan of battle, demanded by the exigencies of the field. Thomas was ordered to move directly against the Ridge. It was three o'clock in the afternoon when he received the order to advance. Four of his divisions, with a front of about two miles and a half, stood facing the Ridge, at a distance of a mile and a quarter from its base. Johnson held the right, Sheridan and Wood the center, and Baird the left. The ground between them and the Ridge was a plain, broken with shallow streams, and thinly covered with patches of thicket and forest. The rebel works along the foot of the hills could be plainly seen, the ground before them having been well cleared to give effective play to the guns. Half-way up the slope was a second line, while the crest was strengthened with continous field-works carrying fifty guns, and defended along the line of Thomas' assault by four veteran divisions.

At half-past three o'clock, at a signal of six guns from Orchard Knob, twenty thousand men, in four lines, swept forward over the plain, deploying somewhat as they advanced, so as to cover three miles of the Ridge. Fifty guns rained shot and shell upon them as they started, and sprinkled them with deadly sleet over all the way. There were many dead and wounded, but no stragglers, as those magnificent waves of battle rolled on. In fifteen minutes they were within range of the galling infantry fire from the lower line of works; in fifteen more they had swept over them along their entire front, and the rebel troops not captured were in full retreat towards their second line above. The orders for the movement contemplated a halt in the first line of works for slight rest, and a re-forming of lines for forward movement; but impatient under the galling fire from above, elated by success, anxious and determined to play their full part in the day's pageant, the front line scarcely halted at the lower works, but, springing over and out of them, began to climb the rough face of the Ridge.

It was five hundred yards to the summit. The general elevation was five hundred feet, and from a point a short distance within the works at the base the slope became precipitous. It was broken by ravines, tangled with fallen timber, strewn with masses of rock, and covered at points with loose stone from the ledges on the crest. Spurs projected from the face of the Ridge at intervals, serving for natural bastions from which field artillery and riflemen swept the intervening curtains of the slope with an enfilading fire. But nothing less than the palisades of Lookout could have stopped that Army of the Cumberland, though Bragg and his thousands above still deemed their position impregnable. All heights were fringed with spectators of that wonderful assault. The guns in the Union works which had covered the first advance were necessarily silent. The sun shone clear on the slopes, and the advancing flags and glittering bayonets marked the rush of the swift ascent. Under the fire of sharp-shooters, color-bearers fell at every point of the line, only to be relieved by other hands eagerly bearing the colors forward. This deadly fire gradually drew each regiment towards its flags, and soon, far as the eye could reach along the slope, the line was transformed into countless wedge-shaped masses, with a flag at the point of each, cleaving their way upward, following the headlong push of the guards bearing the colors. The rebels that had been hurled back from the lower lines were soon driven out of the second parallel, and thence pursued so closely to the summit, that retreating Confederate and the Union flags poured over the whole extended line of works together. There was a sharp hand-to-hand fighting at points, after the crest was gained, and the battle of much spirit on the left, where columns of the enemy, hurrying from Sherman's front, undertook, but without success, to drive Baird back. Bragg and Breckenridge in person barely escaped Sheridan's troops when they crowned the summit. Forty guns and several thousand prisoners were taken in the works. From the first it had been an advance almost wholly without firing. Each successive line of works and the summit were carried with the bayonet. In an hour from the sounding of the signal guns, Bragg had been swept from these dominating positions of a great natural fortress, strengthened by every engineering art, and the sun, which at its rising lighted up that one flag on Lookout, rested at its setting on the countless banners which a stormy army had planted along the crest of Missionary Ridge.

At nightfall Bragg, hotly pursued, was in full retreat, leaving Chattanooga, the most important stronghold in the West, in Union control.

Gen. W. T. Sherman, in closing his report, says:

In reviewing the facts, I must do justice to the men in my command for the patience, cheerfulness, and courage which officers and men have displayed throughout, in battle, on the march, and in camp. For long periods, without regular rations or supplies of any kind, they have marched through mud and over rocks, sometimes barefooted, without a murmur. Without a moment's rest after a march of over four hundred miles, without sleep for three successive nights, we crossed the Tennessee, fought our part of the battle of Chattanooga, pursued the enemy out of Tennessee, and then turned more than a hundred and twenty miles north, and compelled Longstreet to raise the seige of Knoxville, which gave so much anxiety to the whole country. It is hard to realize the importance of these events without recalling the memory of the general feeling which pervaded all minds prior to our arrival. I cannot speak of the Fifteenth Army Corps without seeming vanity; but as I am no longer its commander, I assert that there is no better body of soldiers in America than it. I wish all to feel a just pride in its real honors.

ROSTER ARMY OF THE CUMBERLAND

November, 1863.

Major-General GEORGE H. THOMAS, Commanding.

4th Corps.—Major-General Gordon Granger.
14th Corps.—Major-General John M. Palmer.
Cavalry Corps.—Brigadier-General W. L. Elliott.
Artillery Brigade.—Brigadier-General John M. Brannan.

Major-General JOSEPH HOOKER, Commanding.

11th Corps.—Major-General O. O. Howard.
12th Corps.—Major-General H. W. Slocum.

FOURTH CORPS.

FIRST DIVISION.

Brigadier-General CHARLES CRUFT.

First Brigade.—Col. D. A. Enyart, 1st, 2d Kentucky, 31st, 29th, 81st Indiana, 90th, 101st Ohio, 21st, 38th Illinois, at Bridgeport, Ala.
Second Brigade.—Brig.-Gen. Walter C. Whitaker, 96th, 115th Illinois, 35th, 84th Indiana, 40th, 51st, 99th Ohio, 8th, 21st Kentucky, with Gen. Hooker.
Third Brigade.—Col. William Grose, 9th, 30th, 36th Indiana, 59th, 75th, 84th Illinois, 24th Ohio, 77th Pennsylvania, with Gen. Hooker.
Artillery.—Battery H, 4th United States, Battery M, 4th United States, 5th Indiana.

SECOND DIVISION.

Maj.-Gen. PHIL. H. SHERIDAN.

First Brigade.—Col. Frank Sherman, 36th, 44th, 74th, 73d, 88th Illinois, 24th Wisconsin, 22d Indiana, 2d, 15th Missouri.
Second Brigade.—Brig.-Gen. G. D. Wagner, 100th Illinois, 15th, 40th, 57th, 58th Indiana, 26th, 97th Ohio.
Third Brigade.—Col. C. G. Harker, 54th, 65th, 125th Ohio, 22d, 27th, 42d, 51st, 79th Illinois, 3d Kentucky.
Artillery.—Battery G and M, 1st Missouri, 10th Indiana Battery.

THIRD DIVISION.

Brig.-Gen. THOS. J. WOOD.

First Brigade.—Brig.-Gen. A. Willich, 15th Wisconsin, 8th Kansas, 25th, 35th, 89th Illinois, 32d, 68th Indiana, 15th, 49th Ohio.
Second Brigade.—Brig.-Gen. W. B. Hazen, 1st, 6th, 41st, 93d, 124th Ohio, 5th, 6th, 23d Kentucky, 6th Indiana.
Third Brigade.—Brig.-Gen. Sam. Beatty, 44th, 79th, 86th Indiana, 13th, 19th, 59th Ohio, 9th, 17th Kentucky.
Artillery.—26th Pennsylvania, 6th Ohio, Bridge's Illinois Batteries.

FOURTEENTH CORPS.

FIRST DIVISION.

Brig.-Gen. R. W. JOHNSON.

First Brigade.—Brig.-Gen. W. T. Carlin, 104th Illinois, 10th Wisconsin, 15th Kentucky, 38th, 42d, 88th Indiana, 2d, 33d, 94th Ohio.

Second Brigade.—Col. W. L. Stoughton, 1st and 2d battalion 15th United States, 1st battalion 16th United States, 1st and 2d battalion 18th United States, 1st battalion 19th United States, 69th Ohio, 19th Illinois, 11th Michigan.

Third Brigade.—Brig.-Gen. J. C. Starkweather, 1st, 21st Wisconsin, 78th, 79th Pennsylvania, 24th Illinois, 21st, 74th Ohio, 37th Indiana, in works at Chattanooga.

Artillery.—Battery H, 5th United States, C, 1st Illinois, A, 1st Michigan.

SECOND DIVISION.

Brig.-Gen. JEFF. C. DAVIS.

First Brigade.—Brig.-Gen. D. Morgan, 10th, 60th, 16th, 101st Illinois, 10th Michigan.

Second Brigade.—Brig.-Gen. J. Beatty, 3d, 98th, 108th, 113th, 121st Ohio, 34th, 78th Illinois.

Third Brigade.—Col. O. F. Harmer, 85th, 86th, 110th, 125th Illinois, 52d Ohio, with Gen. Sherman.

Artillery.—Battery I, 2d Illinois, 2d Minnesota Battery, 5th Wisconsin Battery.

THIRD DIVISION.

Brig.-Gen. ABSALOM BAIRD.

First Brigade.—Brig.-Gen. John B. Turchin, 11th, 36th, 31st, 89th, 92d Illinois, 17th Ohio, 82d Indiana.

Second Brigade.—Col. Ferd. Vandeveer, 75th, 87th, 101st Indiana, 35th, 89th, 105th Ohio, 2d Minnesota.

Third Brigade.—Col. E. H. Phelps, 4th, 10th, 18th Kentucky, 14th, 38th Ohio, 10th, 74th Indiana.

Artillery.—Battery I, 4th United States, 7th Indiana Battery, 19th Indiana Battery.

Reserve Artillery.—Batteries A, B, C, F, E, G, M, 1st Ohio, Battery E, 1st Michigan, Battery A, 1st Tennessee, 18th and 20th Ohio Batteries, 3d, 8th and 10th Wisconsin Batteries, 4th, 8th, 11th Indiana Batteries, Battery C, 1st Wisconsin.

CAVALRY CORPS.

FIRST DIVISION.

Col. ED. M. McCOOK.

First Brigade.—Col. A. P. Campbell, 2d Michigan, 9th Pennsylvania, 1st East Tennessee.

Second Brigade.—Col. O. H. LaGrange, 1st Wisconsin, 2d, 4th Indiana, 2d East Tennessee.

Third Brigade.—Col. L. D. Watkins, 4th, 5th, 6th, 7th Kentucky, 18th Indiana Battery.

SECOND DIVISION.

Brig.-Gen. GEO. C. CROOK.

First Brigade.—Col. W. W. Lowe, 4th Michigan, 7th Pennsylvania, 4th United States, 3d Indiana, 5th Iowa.
Second Brigade.—Col. Eli Long, 1st, 3d, 4th, 10th Ohio, 2d Kentucky.
Third Brigade.—Col. A. O. Miller, 17th, 72d Indiana, 92d, 98th, 123d Illinois Mounted Infantry, Chicago Board of Trade Battery.

ELEVENTH CORPS.

FIRST DIVISION.

Brig.-Gen. A. VON STEINWEHR.

First Brigade.—Col. Bushbeck, 27th, 73d Pennsylvania, 134th, 154th New York, 33d New Jersey.
Second Brigade.—Col. O. Smith, 73d. 55th Ohio, 33d Massachusetts, 136th New York.

THIRD DIVISION.

Major-Gen. C. SCHURZ.

First Brigade.—Brig.-Gen. H. Tyndall, 45th, 153d New York, 82d, 61st Ohio, 101st Illinois.
Second Brigade.—Col. W. Krzyranowski, 26th Wisconsin, 58th, 119th, 141st New York.
Third Brigade.—Col. F. Hecker, 80th, 82d Illinois, 75th Pennsylvania, 68th New York.
Artillery.—Battery I, 1st New York, G, 4th United States, I and K, 1st Ohio, 13th New York Battery, with Gen. Sherman.

TWELFTH CORPS.

FIRST DIVISION.

Brig.-Gen. A. S. WILLIAMS.

First Brigade.—Brig.-Gen. J. F. Knipe, 5th, 21st Connecticut, 123d, 145th New York, 3d Maryland, 46th Pennsylvania.
Second Brigade.—Broken up.
Third Brigade.—Brig.-Gen. T. H. Ruger, 27th Indiana, 3d Wisconsin, 2d Massachusetts, 13th New Jersey, 107th, 150th New York.
Artillery.—Battery F, 4th United States, M, 1st New York, B, 2d Kentucky, 9th Ohio Battery. Along communications.

SECOND DIVISION.

Brig.-Gen. JOHN W. GEARY.

First Brigade.—Col. H. Patrick, 5th, 7th, 29th, 66th Ohio, 28th, 147th Pennsylvania.
Second Brigade.—Col. G. A. Cobham, 29th, 109th, 111th Pennsylvania.
Third Brigade.—Col. D. Ireland, 60th, 78th, 102d, 137th, 149th New York.
Artillery.—Battery E, Pennsylvania, Battery K, 5th United States, with Gen. Hooker.
Engineer Brigade.—Brig.-Gen. W. F. Smith, 18th Ohio, 1st, 21st, 22d Michigan.

MAJ.-GEN. WM. T. SHERMAN, COMMANDING ARMY OF THE TENNESSEE.

FIFTEENTH CORPS.

Major-General FRANK P. BLAIR.

FIRST DIVISION.

Brig.-Gen. P. J. OSTERHAUS.

First Brigade.—Brig.-Gen. Chas. R. Woods, 13th Illinois, 3d, 12th, 17th, 27th, 29th, 31st, 32d Missouri, 76th Ohio.

Second Brigade.—Col. James A. Williamson, 4th, 9th, 25th, 26th, 30th, 31st Iowa.

Artillery.—Capt. N. N. Griffiths, Chief of Artillery, 1st Iowa Battery, 1st Missouri Horse Artillery, 4th Ohio Battery, with Gen. Hooker.

SECOND DIVISION.

Brig.-Gen. MORGAN L. SMITH.

First Brigade.—Brig.-Gen. Giles A. Smith, 55th, 116th, 127th Illinois, 6th, 8th Missouri, 57th Ohio, 13th United States (1st Battalion).

Second Brigade.—Brig.-Gen. J. A. J. Lightbourne, 83d Indiana, 30th, 37th, 47th, 54th Ohio, 4th West Virginia.

Artillery.—1st Illinois Light Artillery, Batteries A, B, H.

THIRD DIVISION.

Brig.-Gen. JOHN E. SMITH.

First Brigade.—Brig.-Gen. Ralph P. Buckland, 114th Illinois, 93d Indiana, 72d, 95th Ohio.

Second Brigade.—Brig.-Gen. J. A. Mower, 47th Illinois, 5th Minnesota, 11th Missouri, 8th Wisconsin.

Third Brigade.—Col. James L. Geddes, 8th, 12th, 35th Iowa.

Artillery.—Capt. N. P. Spoor, Chief of Artillery, 1st Illinois Light Artillery, Battery E, 6th Indiana Battery, 2d Iowa Battery.

FOURTH DIVISION.

Brig.-Gen. HUGH EWING.

First Brigade.—Col. John Mason Loomis; 26th Illinois, Lt.-Col. R. A. Gilmore; 90th Illinois, Col. T. O'Meara; 12th Indiana, Lt.-Col. Albert Heath; 100th Indiana, Col. Rube Williams.

Second Brigade.—Brig.-Gen. John M. Corse; 40th Illinois, Major Hiram W. Hall; 103d Illinois, Col. Willard A. Dickerman; 6th Iowa, Lt.-Col. Alex. J. Miller; 15th Michigan, Col. John M. Oliver; 46th Ohio, Col. C. C. Walcutt.

Third Brigade.—Col. Joseph K. Cockerill; 48th Illinois, Lt.-Col. Lucien Greathouse; 97th Indiana, Col. Friend S. Rutherford; 99th Indiana, Col. Robert F. Catterson; 53d Ohio, Col. Wells S. Jones; 70th Ohio, Lt.-Col. D. W. C. Loudon.

Artillery.—Capt. Henry Richardson, Chief of Artillery; 1st Illinois Light Artillery, Battery F, Capt. J. F. Cheeny; 1st Illinois Light Artillery, Battery I, 1st Missouri Light Artillery, Battery D, Lieut. B. Callender.

To illustrate the accuracy that events are recorded at the time of occurrence, also the value of such memorandum and the pleasure and help it would have been to the compiler in preparing this memorial, if the notes which follow could have been as accurately depicted during the Battery's term of service as they are here, in the few happily saved. Colonel Wiedrich kept, up to the time of arriving at Chattanooga, a full diary, but losing it during that campaign, its loss is greatly to be regretted.

Extract From Notes.

Aug. 22, '62.—At Freeman's Ford; was in the center 10 A. M. to 4 P. M. One man killed and four wounded. The one killed was buried near the battle-field; two of the wounded were sent to Alexandria, Va.; two were left in hospital at Harrison Camp, and subsequently taken prisoners.

Aug. 24.—Near Sulphur Springs, from 11 A. M. till 2 P. M.; no loss.

Aug. 25.—At Waterloo Bridge; position near the bridge, from early in the morning until dark. One man slightly wounded, who was sent to Alexandria, Va.

Aug. 29-30.—Battle of Bull Run. 29th, were in position on the right of the Gainesville turnpike from 10 A. M. to 4 P. M., when our ammunition became exhausted, and were obliged to retire for a further supply. This day one officer (Lieut. Schenkelberger) and one enlisted man (Wm. I. Moeller) wounded.

Aug. 30.—The Battery was in reserve until 2 P. M., when we were ordered into a position on a hill to the left of the Gainesville pike. Soon after taking this position the enemy made a desperate charge on our lines, compelling us to fall back to the next hill. This day we had three men wounded, who were sent with the others to the hospital at Alexandria.

May 1, '63.—Battle of Chancellorsville. Went into position on the left of the plank road leading from Fredericksburg to Gordonsville, near South Grove Church, with the 1st brigade, second division, Eleventh Corps; where about 4 P. M., May 2d, the enemy made a sudden attack with overwhelming forces on our right, consisting of the first and third divisions of the Eleventh Corps, which, yielding, was repulsed in disorder, carrying the second with them, until we reached the rifle-pits, which had been built during the afternoon, near Dawdell's Tavern. This day we lost one man killed whom we were obliged to leave upon the field, ten wounded, and two missing; the wounded were sent to Washington, D. C.

May 3-4.—We were in the position near the road leading from Fredericksburg to Germania Ford, with the First Corps. No loss sustained these two days. We then left the field on the evening of the 5th, and returned to Brooks station.

Nov. 24.—Battle of Lookout Mountain, Tennessee. On the 9th inst. we took a position on the summit of a mountain near and west of Lookout Mountain, which position we fortified by building bomb-proofs; during which time the enemy kept up a continued shelling of our position, but without any effect or loss to us, until on the 24th, at 10 A. M., when Gen. Geary's division, Twelfth Army Corps, made the attack on Lookout Mountain on our extreme right. We opened fire on the enemy's rifle-pits near the foot of the mountain with good effect, driving the enemy from their works and up the mountain. This engagement lasted about four hours.

Nov. 25.—We removed the Battery across Lookout Creek, where we took a position at the foot of Lookout Mountain, where we remained several days.

May 15.—Resaca, Ga. Were engaged about two hours without loss.

June 2.—Had two men wounded in a skirmish near Dallas, Ga. On the 16th, 17th, and 18th of June we were heavily engaged with the enemy at Golgotha, Ga.; had one man killed. On the 22d of June, were engaged for about two hours near Culp's house; had one man badly wounded.

June 27.—Were engaged all forenoon near Kennesaw Mountain; had one man killed. June 28th, all day without loss.

July 20.—Battle of Peach Tree Creek. Were engaged for several hours; one man killed and three wounded.

On the 22d of July, at evening, we took a position at about 1,100 yards from the enemy's works in front of Atlanta, under a heavy fire of artillery; had one man wounded during the night. Early in the morning of July 23d, heavy artillery firing commenced, also some skirmishing, when the enemy made an attempt to break our lines, but was handsomely repulsed. The day closed with slow artillery firing. From July 24th to August 24th the Battery was firing at intervals, throwing shells into the city and the enemy's works, during which time we had one officer killed and three men wounded.

Nov. 9.—We had a short skirmish with some of the enemy's cavalry, who retired after firing a few shots, and without damage to us.

Dec. 11.—The Battery took a position on the Savannah River; and on the morning of the 12th, two gunboats of the enemy, the *Mason* and the *Samson*, with the tender *Resolute*, loaded with provisions, came down the river. As soon as they came in range of our guns, we opened fire. After a half hour's firing, they steamed up the river again, leaving the tender in a disabled condition, which was captured by us.

March 16.—Engaged from early in the morning until night with the enemy at Averysboro, N. C., without loss. Also on the 19th, at Bentonville, from 10 A. M. until night, when we had two men captured.

Subsequent to the battle of Lookout Mountain, the record of the Battery may be summed up as follows,—as the official records from the War Department have not at this date been published:

The Battery was assigned to a division of the Twentieth Corps, Army of the Cumberland, to June, 1865, and accompanied Gen. Sherman in his famous " March to the Sea," participating as usual in every contest of any importance in the *Atlanta Campaign, May to September, 1864.* They were in the engagement at Mission Ridge, November 25; operations about Rocky Face Ridge, Tunnel Hill, and Buzzard's Roost, May 5-11, 1864; battle of Resaca, May 13-16; Cassville, May 19-22; battles in the vicinity of Dallas, Pumpkinvine Creek, and Allatoona Hills, May 25 to June 4; New Hope Church, May 27-28; Ackworth Station, June 3-4; operations against Kennesaw Mountain, June 9 to July 2; Pine Mountain, June

14; Lost Mountain, June 15-17; Golgotha, June 16; Culp's Farm, June 22; Assault at Kennesaw, June 27; Marietta, July 3-4; Chattahoochie River, July 6-17; Peach Tree Creek, July 19-20; Siege of Atlanta, July 22 to September 2; *March to the Sea, November 15 to December 10;* Milledgeville, November 22-23; Buffalo Creek, November 25-26; Ogeechee River, November 29; Siege of Savannah, December 10-21; *Campaign of the Carolinas, January to April, 1865;* Roberts Mills, S. C., February 1; Salkehetchie, February 2-3; Orangeburg, February 12-13; Columbia, February 16-17; Chesterfield, March 2; Averysboro, N. C., March 16; battle of Bentonville, March 19-21; occupation of Goldsboro and Raleigh; Bennett's House, April 26; Surrender of Johnston; *March to Washington, D. C., via Richmond, Va.; Grand Review at Washington, D. C., May 24;* and *Mustered Out at Buffalo, N. Y., June 23, 1865.*

Extract from the *Express*, June 10, 1865:

The arrival of Wiedrich's Battery in this city yesterday morning was expected when the dispatch was received from it the previous night. Miller's Band was in waiting for it at the depot, but no general reception was given it, as it was impossible to do so from the brief notice given us of its coming. The members of Taylor Hose Co. No. 1, and Citizens' Hook and Ladder Co. No. 2, had been out to the fire earlier in the morning, formed an escort and accompanied them to Fort Porter, preceded by Miller's Band,—an act of courtesy which calls forth universal commendation. The Battery numbers 146 men, and they seem in appearance all that their reputation has represented—efficient and brave. Their officers are as follows:

    Lieut. W. L. Scott, commanding.
    Lieut. I. Adle.
    Lieut. S. M. Hood.

Captain C. Winegar, upon whom the command devolved after the promotion of Col. Wiedrich, is on detached service, consequently Lieut. Scott commands the Battery.

Previous to the report of the Gettysburg Monument Commissioners of this State, the members of the Battery had taken no active measures to keep up an organization. But in August, 1888, as will be seen by the following circular, a call for a meeting was had, to take measures for the dedication of their monument at Gettysburg:

WIEDRICH'S BATTERY—A MEETING TO ARRANGE FOR THE DEDICATION OF A GETTYSBURG MONUMENT.

HEADQUARTERS SOCIETY OF BATTERY I,
FIRST REGIMENT NEW YORK LIGHT ARTILLERY,
BUFFALO, August 8, 1888.

Dear Comrades—By an act of the Legislature of the State of New York, an appropriation has been made for a monument for each command, regiment, or battery who fought in the battle of Gettysburg in July, 1863, in honor of the surviving members of said regiments or batteries, and in memory of those who met their death on the battle-field.

Accordingly, our (Wiedrich's) Battery has ordered a monument, which is under construction at the present time, and which has to be placed at Gettysburg in the month of May, 1889, the date not being fixed yet.

We therefore have called a meeting to be held in Buffalo, N. Y., September 20, 1888, at Metropolitan Hall, 551 Main street, for the purpose of making suitable arrangements for the dedication of said monument on the battle-field of Gettysburg in May next.

In order to enable us to make the necessary arrangements in regard to transportation, etc., we kindly request you to signify your intention and willingness to participate at the dedication, either by attending this next meeting or by forwarding us a letter.

As this is the first reunion of the members of our Battery since the war, we hope and would be pleased to see every comrade, who is able, present at this occasion, as it may perhaps be the last meeting.

COL. M. WIEDRICH,
LIEUT. J. SCHENKELBERGER,
LIEUT. C. SCHMITT,
A. SCHELL.

J. HEHR, *Secretary.*
Address, 306 Carlton St., Buffalo, N. Y.

Between this date and that of the following March, several meetings were held regarding the matter of dedication. Major John M. Farquhar, a gallant soldier of the war of the Rebellion, and our Representative in Congress, consented to deliver an oration upon the occasion.

The means for the transportation of the survivors of the Battery was next in order, and accordingly a petition to the Common Council of this city was decided upon, asking for a sufficient sum to defray the expense. It was presented at the meeting of March 18th, and was duly referred to the Committee on Finance:

BUFFALO, March 18, 1889.

The undersigned, members of Wiedrich's Battery Association, having been appointed a committee to solicit from your Honorable Body an appropriation of there hundred dollars to enable the indigent members of our Association to be present at Gettysburg on the 20th day of May next to take part in the services of unveiling the monument erected by the State of New York on the site occupied by our Battery during the Battle of Gettysburg, July 1, 2, and 3, 1863, do earnestly request that you grant their petition.

The position held by us during those three memorable days was on Cemetery Ridge, near the cemetery overlooking the town. General Howard in his official report makes special mention of our achievement, and says: "These guns did most excellent service. At 4.30 P. M. the columns of the enemy reached Cemetery Hill. He made a single attempt to turn our right, ascending the slope northeast of Gettysburg. His line was instantly broken by Wiedrich's Battery, in position on the heights."

It will be a great pleasure to all the survivors of this noble old battery, if they are again permitted to visit the spot where many of their comrades gave up their lives in defense of their country that this Nation might live, and we sincerely hope your Honorable Body will make it possible for all to be present, and cannot but think your action will meet the approval of your several constituencies.

Respectfully sumbitted,

Col. M. Wiedrich,
J. Schenkelberger,
Philip Bachert,
Jacob Hehr,
Adam Schell,
Committee.

Referred to the Committee on Finance.

On the 21st of the same month, at the next meeting of the Council, the following report was submitted and adopted:

Reports of Standing Committees.

Ald. Hutchinson, from the Committee on Finance, reported in favor of the adoption of the following resolution:

That a warrant be directed drawn on the Fourth of July Fund in favor of Col. M. Wiedrich, for the sum of three hundred dollars, to defray the expenses of the indigent members of the Wiedrich Battery Association to Gettysburg, on the occasion of the unveiling of the monument in memory of said battery.

Adopted.

Of course it was not proper to vote this sum to any deserving charity out of a fund set apart to any particular purpose, and if it were allowable, the precedent would not be a good one.

The *Express* of March 25th had the following editorial:

Patriotic But Improper.

The Common Council has appropriated three hundred dollars to aid survivors of Wiedrich's Battery to revisit Gettysburg.

Mayor Grover Cleveland got almost his first start in public life by vetoing just such a patriotic but improper scheme as this. If there is no legal fund for the celebration of Decoration Day, of what avail is the Council's gratuity to the old artillerymen?

The *Evening News* of the 27th had the following communication, which was handed in early on the 26th:

It Is Patriotic, Anyway.

Editor Evening News—In the *Express* of this morning you may read the following:

"PATRIOTIC BUT IMPROPER.

"The Common Council has appropriated three hundred dollars to aid survivors of Wiedrich Battery to revisit Gettysburg.

"Mayor Grover Cleveland got almost his first start in public life by vetoing just such a patriotic but improper scheme as this. If there is no legal fund for the celebration of Decoration Day, of what avail is the Council's gratuity to the old artillerymen?"

Wiedrich Battery was recruited in this city in 1861. It was the first military organization of this city to offer its services to the Governor for defense of the State, and although it was recruited from among the German element of this city, it was scarcely mentioned by the local papers until its departure in October of that year for the seat of war.

Beside other engagements, it took part in that memorable contest of the first, second and third of July, 1863, at Gettysburg, and was the only battery in that contest representing the City of Buffalo. In Steinwehr's division on Cemetery Hill, under General Howard, it helped the defeat of Early's division, and which repulse was so disheartening that that point was abandoned and the attack was made more to the west, threatening the divisions of Hancock and Sedgwick, and also assisted by its guns in repulsing the famous charge of Pickett's division.

The State of New York, in appreciating its services, have donated the sum of one thousand five hundred dollars with which to erect a monument to their heroism. If the action of the Council is an illegal one, I am sure the survivors of that gallant battery would not wish to touch a cent of the amount donated them in order to convey its disabled members to that historic field, and I will guarantee, provided the same is declined by them, to raise a sum equal to that donated, so that, as in the former time, no obligation need be had, and also that the Fourth of July money may not be diverted from its legitimate design, namely: for fireworks and boat-racing.

Cyrus K. Remington.

Buffalo, March 26, 1889.

PHILIP BACHERT,
Sergeant Battery I, First New York Light Artillery.

THE NEW YORK
PUBLIC LIBRARY

ASTOR, LENOX AND
TILDEN FOUNDATIONS
R   L

The following is from an editorial in the *Commercial* of March 26th:

Raise It By Subscription!

While the Council is justified, and will be supported by public sentiment, in appropriating money for the relief of veterans of the late war who are unable to take care of themselves, it is not justified in appropriating money for excursion expenses. Yesterday three hundred dollars were appropriated to assist survivors of Wiedrich's Battery to visit Gettysburg. We sympathize with the patriotic objects of the excursion; at the same time this is not a legitimate purpose to which to apply the public money. The old soldiers, or the G. A. R., have no warmer or devoted friend than is the *Commercial*, but when they ask the Council to provide money for excursion expenses, we think they are going a little too far. This money should be raised by public subscription. The *Commercial* will cheerfully contribute twenty-five dollars for the purpose. Next!

At the meeting of the Common Council April 8th, the following communication was received from the Mayor:

City and County Hall, in Common Council,
Buffalo, Monday, April 8, 1889, at 2 o'clock, p. m.

Present—William Summers, President of the Council, and Ald. Adams, Baldwin, Barnum, Beck, Bradley, Cannon, Davy, Denner, Drake, Fisher, Franklin, Hutchinson, Kennedy, Knepper, Kreitner, McMaster, Ramsperger, Scheu, Spang, Trautmann, White, Williamson, Wurtz, Young—25.

Absent—Ald. Busch—1.

The minutes of the last session were approved.

FROM THE MAYOR.

Buffalo, April 8, 1889.

At a meeting of your Honorable Body, held March 25th, a resolution was adopted, upon the report of the Committee on Finance, directing a warrant drawn on the Fourth of July Fund in favor of Col. M. Wiedrich for the sum of three hundred dollars to defray the expenses of the indigent members of the Wiedrich Battery Association to Gettysburg, on the occasion of the unveiling of the monument in memory of said battery.

The Fourth of July Fund, so called, is a fund created by placing in the annual estimates and raising by general tax a sum not exceeding five thousand dollars for the celebration of the Fourth of July and the reception of distinguished persons.

Section 8, of Title XVI. of the Charter, provides that "when the city shall borrow or raise money for any particular purpose it shall be applied only to that purpose; and every alderman who shall vote to appropriate it to a different purpose, and every officer who shall knowingly assist in a misappropriation of such money, shall be guilty of a misdemeanor, and on conviction thereof shall be disqualified from holding any office in the city."

Aside from this legal obligation, we are bound by the duties of our respective offices, as servants of the City of Buffalo, to disburse its money only for the purpose of government and a proper maintenance of the dignity of the city; and with all due respect to the surviving members of Wiedrich's Battery, and the patriotic occasion for which this money is asked, we have not in my opinion the right, nor is it proper, that we should thus appropriate any sum out of the city treasury.

The resolution is therefore returned without approval.

PHILIP BECKER, *Mayor*.

Received and filed.

BUFFALO, N. Y., April 8, 1889.

Dear Comrade: You are hereby requested to attend a meeting to be held in Buffalo, April 17, 1889, at 7.30 P. M., at Miller's (Harmonia) Hall, 264 Genesee street, for the purpose of making arrangements for the Dedication of the Monument to be erected for Wiedrich's Battery at Gettysburg on May 19, 1889.

In order to make the necessary arrangements, we kindly request you to attend this meeting, or signify your intention by forwarding us a letter, as it is necessary to know the exact number of comrades who will participate.

COLONEL WIEDRICH.
LIEUT. J. SCHENKELBERGER.
LIEUT. C. SCHMITT.
A. SCHELL.

JACOB HEHR, *Secretary.*
Address, 306 Carlton street, Buffalo, N. Y.

April 9th, in the editorial of the *Express*, is the following appeal:

COME, FELLOW-PATRIOTS!

Of course Mayor Becker has vetoed the grant of three hundred dollars to the poor survivors of Wiedrich's Battery who want to revisit Gettysburg. He could not lawfully do otherwise, and every alderman who voted for the appropriation knew as much. The Council's action was not prompted so much by charity or patriotism as by a desire to put the Mayor in a hole.

But no member of that gallant command who wishes to see the monument of its achievements, which has been set up on that glorious field, should be denied the privilege. Let us have a public subscription to raise that three hundred dollars and as much more as may be needed! The *Express* will contribute its share, and will also take charge of other contributions.

To keep the ball rolling, this from the *Commercial*, same day:

FOLLOWING THE "COMMERCIAL'S" LEAD.

Two weeks ago to-day the *Commercial* said: "While the Council is justified, and will be supported by public sentiment, in appropriating money for the relief of veterans of the late war who are unable to take care of themselves, it is not justified in appropriating money for excursion expenses. Yesterday three hundred dollars were appropriated to assist survivors of Wiedrich's Battery to visit Gettysburg. We sympathize with the patriotic objects of the excursion; at the same time this is not a legitimate purpose to which to apply the public money. The old soldiers, or the G. A. R., have no warmer or more devoted friend than is the *Commercial*, but when they ask the Council to provide money for excursion expenses, we think they are going a little too far. This money should be raised by public subscription. The *Commercial will cheerfully contribute twenty-five dollars for the purpose. Next!"*

Mayor Becker is only too happy to take a hint from the *Commercial*, so he yesterday sent to the Council a veto of the above appropriation. The money will be easily raised. The *Commercial* headed the list with twenty-five dollars, and the amount wanted will be on hand in a few hours. This is the proper way of raising the fund, and to have raised it by appropriation would have been a bad precedent. The Mayor acted wisely in complying with the *Commercial's* suggestion, and he will doubtless be only too happy to follow the *Commercial's* example also in subscribing twenty-five dollars.

Again from the *Express*, April 10th:

FOR WIEDRICH'S BATTERY—ITS POOR SURVIVORS WILL BE PROVIDED WITH FUNDS TO GO TO GETTYSBURG.

The *Express* of yesterday contained the following editorial article:

"Of course Mayor Becker has vetoed the grant of three hundred dollars to the poor survivors of Wiedrich's Battery who want to revist Gettysburg. He could not lawfully do otherwise, and every alderman who voted for the appropriation knew as much. The Council's action was not prompted so much by charity or patriotism as by a desire to put the Mayor in a hole."

"But no member of that gallant command who wishes to see the monument of its achievements, which has been set up on that glorious field, should be denied the privilege. Let us have a public subscription to raise that three hundred dollars and as much more as may be needed! The *Express* will contribute its share, and will also take charge of other contributions."

Cyrus K. Remington has been industriously circulating an appeal, with this result to date:

Cyrus K. Remington	$10
John Greiner	10
Charles Greiner	10
Philip Becker	20
James D. Warren's Sons	25
The Morning Express	25
E. G. Spaulding	25
P. P. Pratt	10
George Bleistein	10
George W. Hayward	5
E. A. Georger	5

An afternoon paper yesterday said: "The Mayor acted wisely in complying with the *Commercial's* suggestion, and he will doubtless be only too happy to follow the *Commercial's* example also in subscribing twenty-five dollars." In point of fact, the Mayor subscribed before the *Commercial* did.

Other gifts may be left with Mr. Remington, the *Express*, or at the Erie County Savings Bank, where the money is deposited.

From the *Courier*, April 15th:

WIEDRICH'S BATTERY — THE EFFORT TO SEND INDIGENT MEMBERS TO GETTYSBURG — HISTORY OF THE BATTERY DURING THE CIVIL WAR — NAMES OF THE GALLANT SURVIVORS WHO LIVE IN BUFFALO — THREE HUNDRED DOLLARS RAISED THUS FAR, BUT MORE NEEDED.

The citizens who have collected subscriptions to aid in sending the indigent members of Wiedrich's Battery to Gettysburg this spring have been successful in obtaining about three hundred dollars.

A call has been issued for a meeting of the survivors of the Battery, to be held April 17, at 7.30 P. M. at Miller's Hall, to make arrangements for the dedication of the monument.

Wiedrich's Battery was formed in August, 1861, as Battery I of the First New York Artillery, but during a greater part of the war it acted as a separate organization. It was composed entirely of men of German birth or parentage. At its organization it had one hundred and forty men, and was officered as follows: Captain, Michael Wiedrich, who had been captain of the battery attached to the 65th Regiment; first lieutenants, Nicholas Sahm and Diedrich Erdmann; second lieutenants, Christopher Schmitt and Jacob Schenkelberger.

The Battery left Buffalo for Virginia October 16, 1861. It was attached to Blenker's division and was in camp near Washington during the following winter.

In the campaign of 1862 it was severely tried. At the battles of Cross Keys, June 8, and Freeman's Ford, August 22, it lost several men, killed and wounded. Second Bull Run was its first hard fight. Lieut. Schenkelberger and thirteen men were wounded out of the one hundred engaged. Five of the six guns in the Battery were disabled, and two of the carriages had to be left on the field. By desperate exertions the guns were saved. During the remainder of the year the Battery was in minor engagements.

At Chancellorsville, the following year, the Battery distinguished itself. When Hooker was obliged to fall back, Capt. Wiedrich had to leave behind two of the guns. At one of them all the men but one had been shot down, and at the other four horses were killed. Four men were killed and fourteen wounded.

The Battery never seemed to miss a battle. At Gettysburg three men were killed, and Lieuts. Sahm and Stock and seven men were wounded.

In September it was sent to Nashville and to the vicinity of Chattanooga. It was present at the bloody battles of Lookout Mountain and Missionary Ridge in November, but escaped loss.

Early in the following February Capt. Wiedrich was promoted to be Lieutenant-Colonel of the 15th New York Heavy Artillery. Lieut. Sahm died soon after his promotion to be captain of the Battery, and was succeeded by Capt. Charles Winegar. The Battery was with Sherman on his great march to the sea, and thence northward, and participated in nearly every battle on the route. At Lost Mountain, June 4, 1864, two men were wounded; at Ackworth Station one was killed; at Kennesaw Mountain one was killed and one wounded; at Peach Tree Creek, July 20, one was killed and five wounded; at the siege of Atlanta, Lieut. Henchen was killed and two men were mortally wounded. In 1865 the Battery was mustered out.

There are about forty-five survivors of the Battery living in Buffalo and vicinity. They are: Col. Michael Wiedrich, Lieut. Jacob Schenkelberger, Lieut. Christopher Schmitt, Lieut. Warren L. Scott, Lieut. Diedrich Erdmann, Philip Bachert, Jacob Hehr, Jacob Hirt, Adam Schell, John Stortz, Cirach Diebold, Peter Kehl, John Kappel, James Winspear, Samuel Vogel, Joseph Debel, Christopher Fahrnholz, Henry Fuerschbach, Jacob Gabel, John Garbe, Wellington Miner, Philip Strang, Francis Herrman, Henry Kraner, George K. Frazier, William I. Moeller, Charles Schwartz, Charles Schmidt, John Horn, Henry Wise, George Schreier, Nicholas Stahl, Philip Stemler, Louis Vetter, William Snearly, George Burghard,

Philip Uebelhoer, Philip Arras, Christian Horni, Robert Burger, John Messinger, Nicholas Mangold, William Braun, Charles Buchlieter, Matthew Keller, Gustav Gabel, Peter Brandel, George Bair, Michael Duffner, Michael Pflug, Christian Schmidt, Fred Smith, Fred Schlem, John G. Schneider, Andrew Seifert, Andrew Zimmer, Joseph Lechtenberger, George Volk, John Weber, Jacob Klipfel, John Zuber, George F. Schwartz, Charles Segor, Jacob Schmidt, and Henry Klee.

From the *Daily Courier :*

The Mayor yesterday vetoed the resolution of the Council voting three hundred dollars to enable indigent members of Wiedrich's Battery Association to attend the unveiling of their monument at Gettysburg. In these circumstances certain of the Aldermen yesterday afternoon did a very graceful thing. Acting on a suggestion made by Ald. Hutchinson some weeks ago, Ald. Beck circulated in the Council Chamber a subscription paper which before the adjournment of the meeting footed up over two hundred dollars of the required sum. The paper itself points a moral, for it shows that those who talk the loudest for veterans are not the most ready with needed cash. Seven Democratic Aldermen signed with alacrity, but only four Republican councilmen could be induced to subscribe. The list is headed by Aldermen Hutchinson, Beck, Scheu, and Drake with subscriptions of twenty-five dollars each ; the other subscribers of smaller sums include Aldermen Cannon, Kennedy, Summers, Davy, Kreitner, Knepper, and Denner. The names of the Hon. Jacob Stern, Mr. Reimann, Commissioner of Public Buildings, and City Engineer Mann also appear on the list. The veterans need not be alarmed about getting the sum asked. Without such aid it is stated that only four or five of the Battery would be able to attend the unveiling of the monument which has been erected to perpetuate the memory of their valor.

The writer, pending the veto, had offered his services in assisting to raise the necessary funds to enable all the members to attend the dedication of their monument. They were accepted, and he was also requested to prepare a historical account, to be read at that time.

From the *Express*, of April 18th:

They Will All Go.

Survivors of Wiedrich's Battery held a meeting at Miller's Hall last evening, the purpose being to see how many would attend the unveiling of the monument at Gettysburg next month. There were thirty-five survivors present who had announced their intention to go anyway, and after considering the matter it was decided that the money for the remaining five would be raised. The secretary stated that he had received letters from members living in other parts of the country, stating that they would meet their old comrades at the old battle-ground. The Battery will leave here on Sunday, May 19th, and will dedicate their monument on Monday. Congressman Farquhar and Cyrus K. Remington will be the orators on that occasion.

From the *Express*, May 12th:

The Wiedrich Excursion to Gettysburg.

Arrangements for the excursion of Wiedrich's Battery and their friends to Gettysburg for the purpose of unveiling and dedicating their monument are now completed. The excursion will leave Buffalo on Sunday, the 19th inst., and go via Harrisburg and Carlisle, arriving at Gettysburg at ten o'clock Monday morning.

The dedication will take place that afternoon about two o'clock, after which the party will go over the field in carriages in charge of Capt. James T. Long, the battle-field guide, who will explain all points of interest. There are now over two hundred memorial shafts or tablets, all works of art, erected on the field, marking positions held during the three days of the fight, by the different regiments and batteries. The exercises will take place on the field of Gettysburg, the monument having been erected on the spot occupied by Wiedrich's Battery during the famous engagement. The programme will include an oration by the Hon. John M. Farquhar, an address by Cyrus K. Remington of this city, and the formal presentation of the monument to the Commission by Col. Wiedrich.

Following is a list of the members residing in this city intending to visit Gettysburg the 20th inst.:

Colonel Michael Wiedrich; Lieutenants Christopher Schmitt, Jacob Schenkelberger, George F. Schwartz, and Diedrich Erdmann; Sergeants John Garbe, Philip Bachert, Cirach Dieboldt, and Jacob Hirt; and Privates John Messinger, Adam Schell, Jacob Hehr, John Stortz, Henry Feuersbach, Philip Strang, Frank Herrmann, Philip Stemler, George Burghard, Philip Arras, Nicholas Mangold, William Brown, Matthew Keller, Jacob Schmitt, Andrew Siebert, Andrew Zimmer, Joseph Lichtenberger, George Baer, Henry Klee, Charles Buchleiter, Louis Vetter, Henry Kramer, Christian Horni, Nicholas Stahl, George Knorr, George Volk, and William Miller.

Three other members, residing respectively in Michigan, Pennsylvania, and South Carolina, have signified their intention to be present at the ceremonies. There will also be quite a number of friends, among whom are Ald. Beck and family, ex-Ald. Miller, Col. Wiedrich's daughter, and others who have signified their intention of going if possible.

The friends of the Battery have responded very liberally to the call for help, but still need a little more to help them out. This being the last call, it is hoped our citizens will respond.

From the *Express*, May 19th:

GOING TO GETTYSBURG — SURVIVORS OF WIEDRICH'S BATTERY WILL LEAVE TO-DAY FOR THE BATTLE-FIELD.

To-day the gallant survivors of Wiedrich's Battery will leave Buffalo for the purpose of unveiling and dedicating their monument on the battle-field of Gettysburg. They will go via Harrisburg and Carlisle, reaching Gettysburg at ten o'clock to-morrow morning.

From the *Express* (editorial), May 20th:

WHERE ONCE THEY STOOD.

More than a quarter of a century ago a stalwart body of brave young men left Buffalo for the fair Southern country. They were going where the sweetness of summer is not cut short by the rigorous winter of our lake country, and where sunshine and flowers and the warmth of the generous South offer a genial welcome to the visitor from the colder North. But little thought those young Buffalonians of such things. Their errand was a dreadful one. They went to spread fire and blood through that fair region. They went to serve grape and canister and shell and solid shot to the brazen dogs of war that growled and howled and roared all through four years of fratricidal strife. They went, not because they loved to see humanity mangled by shrieking missiles, or to witness the burning of homes and the desolation of the land, but because from that Southern country had come tidings that the flag which stands for all we hold dear in America had fallen before the cannon of those who were sworn to uphold and protect it. And though many of that particular group of young men were born under a foreign standard, there rushed not to the front in those dark days any more patriotic little band of Americans than those who formed Wiedrich's Battery.

The sons of many of those men are older to-day than their fathers were then. The years that dragged so heavily by during that momentous struggle have sprung forward since with ever-hastening steps. History has been made at lightning speed, and with strong, bold strokes. But nowhere upon its scroll is carved a more worthy roster or a fairer record than that of Wiedrich's Battery. And thirty-two bent, grizzled and wrinkled men marched away from Buffalo yesterday—the remnant of that noble corps—to find once more the spot where their gallant battery stood during the awful three days at Gettysburg, and to mark it, that it may not be forgotten when they are gone. Perchance, too, the old men of Wiedrich's Battery shall find the names of well-loved comrades marking certain lowly green tents in that quiet hillside camp where an august host sleeps in undisturbed peace, awaiting the only reveille that can awaken them. And, if so, they will not be forgotten when their surviving comrades—only thirty-two of them—gather where once all stood together and served their smoking guns.

Nor will Buffalo forget them. Our city has many memorials on that field. Her sons sleep there. They went from home at various times and in different commands. But, so long as "the mystic chords of memory" stretch from battle-field to hearth, the Buffalo dead at Gettysburg will never be forgotten.

From the *Courier*, May 20th:

OFF FOR GETTYSBURG—DEPARTURE OF WIEDRICH'S BATTERY FOR THE FAMOUS BATTLE-GROUND.

To the sound of patriotic airs, played by Young's Band, the gallant remnant of Wiedrich's Battery marched to the Central-Hudson station yesterday afternoon and took the train for Gettysburg. There were but thirty-three of them, but Lieut. Schmitt walked as proudly at their head as if he had been leading a brigade. Col. Wiedrich did not appear till just before 3.30 o'clock, when they were ready to start.

"We are going to unveil our new monument at Gettysburg," said Lieut. Schmitt to a reporter. "We will go down on the Pennsylvania road through Harrisburg, and will reach Gettysburg at 9.30 o'clock to-morrow morning. At two o'clock the monument will be dedicated. Congressman Farquhar will deliver an oration, to which Mr. Cyrus K. Remington will add a fitting speech. The monument is a beauty and stands on the spot where we made it lively for the Johnnies.

"After the dedication we will go over the whole battle-field in carriages, guided by Capt. Long.

"We will put up at the Yuengling House, and the most of us will be back Wednesday evening, though a few may go on to Washington and spend a week or ten days reviewing the Capital.

"Quite a number of our friends, as you can plainly see, are going with us, and if the weather is fair, we expect to have a great time."

From the *Freie Presse*, May 20th:

The survivors of Wiedrich's Battery started yesterday for the battle-field of Gettysburg, in order to unveil the monument which has been erected in memory of their comrades fallen there. This morning at ten o'clock they arrived there; at two o'clock this afternoon the ceremony takes place. Maj. John M. Farquhar delivers the oration, supplemented by Cyrus K. Remington with an historical paper. In addition to the members who live here and accompany the party, three members who live in Pennsylvania, Michigan and

South Carolina, respectively, are expected to be present at the ceremony of dedication. Many friends of the Battery also accompany the party.

The veterans marched, with Young's Band at their head, to the depot of the New York Central Railroad, taking Genesee and Main to Exchange street, the band playing patriotic airs on the way. Col. Wiedrich and Lieut. Schenkelberger were in a coach, Phil Bachert commanded, John Garbe carried a new flag, a facsimile of the one used by the Battery. The veterans looked well and seemed intent on having a good time.

From the *Express*, May 20th:

GONE TO GETTYSBURG — THE GALLANT OLD SURVIVORS OF WIEDRICH'S BATTERY LEFT YESTERDAY AFTERNOON.

About thirty-two survivors of Wiedrich's Battery left yesterday afternoon for Gettysburg to unveil and dedicate a monument on the battle-field. The veterans, headed by Young's Band, marched to the Central station, and though the step of the gallant ex-fighters were not as firm or elastic as when they left Buffalo during the war, their hearts were lighter, and vivid recollections of dark days and hard experiences at Gettysburg induced a lively gait for men of their age, as they marched down Main and Exchange streets to the music of "Marching Through Georgia."

Capt. Michael Wiedrich was with his boys, though he was obliged to ride in a carriage with Lieut. Schenkelberger and give Phil Bachert the honor of commanding. Sergt. John Garbe carried a handsome new silk standard of white and blue, bearing the name of the Battery and being a fac-simile of the standard which the Sergeant carried subsequently in many battles.

"It don't look much as our standard did when we left down there," said the Sergeant, and the member recalled how the standard was riddled by bullets, and laughed as he said that the buffalo's head painted on it was pretty well shot up. "I'm glad that I'm to carry this new standard," said the Sergeant, "and that I'm able to go with the boys to again look over that field." The veterans began to recall incidents and story-telling was rife while they were waiting for the call "all aboard," and in more than one pair of eyes there was noted a mist, and down more than one wrinkled cheek a tear sped as a hearty grasp of the hand or some recalled event awoke memories of events, in which those present took a part, or in which some one of the boys was engaged, but was left behind on the field.

Several of the veterans had their wives or other members of their families with them. Ald. Beck and wife were also in the party. The Battery will reach Gettysburg in time for the dedication, which is to occur this afternoon. The Hon. John M. Farquhar is to deliver the oration and Mr. C. K. Remington will also deliver an address.

Accompanying the veterans were the following friends: Alderman August Beck and Mrs. Beck, Henry J. Fox (late 21st N. Y. Vols.) and Mrs. Fox, W. E. Litz and Mrs. Litz, Mrs. John Kappel, Mrs. Adam Schell, Miss Nettie Wiedrich, Miss Wilhelmina Schmitt, Miss Elizabeth Bachert, Warren A. Woodson, M. D., late of Muhlenberger's 4th U. S. Artillery at Battle of Gettysburg, John Irlbacker, late Captain Co. F, 65th Regt. N. G., in campaign of '63, John McAnally, late Captain Co. I, 155th N. Y. Vols., in campaign of '63, Wm. P. Gorges, U. G. Mease, Edward Schuesler, John Messinger, Jr., and Cyrus K. Remington; all of this city, with the exception of Mr. and Mrs. John Kappel, now residing at Milwaukee, Wis., and Mr. Geo. F. Schwartz of South Carolina.

From the *Daily Times*, May 20th:

ON THE BATTLE-FIELD—THE SURVIVORS OF WIEDRICH'S BATTERY RETURN TO GETTYSBURG TO UNVEIL THE MONUMENT TO THEIR DEAD COMRADES.

Wiedrich's Battery left yesterday for Gettysburg to unveil their new monument at that place. They expect to arrive at Gettysburg at 9.30 this morning and will dedicate the monument at two o'clock this afternoon. Congressman Farquhar will deliver an oration and Cyrus K. Remington will read an address. The members expect to return to Buffalo on Wednesday evening.

From the Buffalo *Courier:*

The surviving members of Wiedrich's Battery, which was raised in this city in 1861, known later as Battery I, First New York Light Artillery, numbering thirty-two, and accompanied by friends, making the total forty-eight, left Buffalo on the afternoon of Sunday, May 19, by the New York Central railroad to Canandaigua ; thence by the Northern Central railroad, in charge of B. P. Fraser, General Contracting Agent for the company, for Gettysburg, for the purpose of dedicating the monument lately erected upon the place occupied by the Battery on Cemetery Hill during the memorable days of July, 1863.

The weather, which had been unusually warm, changed about one hour previous to the departure to a violent storm of rain, which followed the excursionists to Gettysburg, and stuck to them while there.

Upon arrival near Gettysburg, the party was met by Major Long, an official guide of the battle-field, accompanied by Doctor Jerome B. Greene, who was attached to the division as Surgeon. At the second Bull Run battle to him was assigned the painful duty of amputating the leg of Lieut. Schenkelberger at that time; also the arm of Sergt. William I. Moeller, which was shattered by the same shot.

Major Long advised the immediate performance of the dedicatory services, on account of the uncertainty of the continuance of fair weather then prevailing. It was fortunate that his advice was taken, as in the afternoon the rain was incessant.

The monument dedicated stands upon East Cemetery Hill, in the space between the four lunettes of the Battery, and is one of the finest positions upon this portion of the field. The material is of granite with cap-stone, surmounted by five cannon-balls; at corners pillars of polished stone. In the front facing the west a large bronze tablet is inserted, representing a gun in action, surrounded by artillerymen and officers. It has above in the apex an oval bronze with the coat-of-arms of this State, also the corps badge. On the east side a tablet records the casualties during the action. The monument is about twelve feet in height, and nobly reflects upon the generosity of the State of New York.

Col. Wiedrich having formed the veterans in line on the east of the monument facing the west, the ceremonies of the occasion were opened by the following address by Cyrus K. Remington:

FRIENDS AND COMRADES:

We assemble here to-day from distant portions of this great country to dedicate the monument erected by a generous State to the memory of those who contended for a grand principle.

The silent witnesses which we behold around us rest upon the places cemented by the life-blood of nearly a thousand of the sons of the Empire State, and more than twenty thousand in addition from other loyal States of the Union tell eloquently of the gratitude of a re-united people and of the obligations due from them to true heroism. Here to-day, in the name of freedom and equality, we give thanks for the inestimable privileges enjoyed by us as a Nation.

Comrades, twenty-six years ago you stood upon this hill, this very spot, to repel an enemy who was seeking to destroy this Union —brother against brother, a fratricidal contest. Those who yielded up their lives rest peacefully here. Well may we envy them their glory, for it is imperishable, and their memory shall be held in grateful remembrance.

No Cæsar returning from his conquests could have vied with you, for in after years the Nation will say of you: " He was at Gettysburg," and your badges will become more honored and cherished as the years roll by.

Comrades, I have an interest in this victorious army. My only brother was the Adjutant of the Third Michigan Infantry, and in that division which successfully opposed the famous charge of Gen. Pickett.

A recital of your gallant deeds has lately been given through the press. Let me briefly recount it:

Your baptism by fire was at Cross Keys, then at Waterloo Bridge, the second Bull Run, Chancellorsville, and at *this* place; and when in that desperate charge of Gen. Early's, who had sworn that he would take and hold these hills, did he with his "Louisiana Tigers" accomplish the feat? And after the guns were so heated by rapid firing that you were unable to use them, what did you do? Run away? No; you stood your ground, beating back the foe with ramrods and whatever came to hand—a not very artistic style of fighting, but effectual. These same men you had met at Chancellorsville a short time previous, and after this repulse they were heard to say that you must have been the same Dutchmen of the Eleventh Corps that they had encountered at that place. Do you recall the "Battle in the Clouds" upon Lookout Mountain? At Allatoona, where Gen. Corse with a few gallant men held at bay a large force of the enemy, and when Sherman heard of his situation he said: "If Gen. Corse is in command he will hold it—I know the man," and immediately signaled him to "Hold the Fort;" at Lost Mountain, Missionary Ridge, Ackworth Station, Kennesaw Mountain, Peach Tree Creek, Louisville, Millen, Savannah, Fayetteville, Bentonville, Goldsboro, and Raleigh; through plains and swamps, across streams and over mountains, you followed your great leader to the finish.

All honor to you and all soldiers of the Union. Providence has generously lengthened your days that you might behold this joyous occasion. You now hear no roar of hostile cannon or call to repeated assault, see no mixed volumes of smoke or flame, no dead or dying. All these you have witnessed, and now a company of sincere friends greet you and thank you in the name of liberty for these heroic deeds.

In the past ages of the world's history the admiration of the people for their military heroes has sought expression in costly monuments. Now the disposition is to commemorate the virtues and services of its citizen soldiery, upon whom the brunt and burden of our Civil War mainly fell, and the corner-stone of that fabric which the leaders of the rebellion sought to erect on human bondage is forever crushed, and bright days of a glorious future are

ADAM SCHELL,
Battery I, First New York Light Artillery.

THE NEW YORK
PUBLIC LIBRARY

ASTOR, LENOX AND
TILDEN FOUNDATIONS

before us to make us a happy nation. These columns will turn to dust, time will with its finger erase all impress from this crumbling stone, but the fame of those heroes remains evermore.

Comrades, it would have befitted the occasion had you been permitted to have with you the colors you carried in that campaign; but their custodian, the State of New York, has so honored them that by an act passed by the Legislature it took charge of them, and, to insure their safety, a clause was inserted which forbids their ever leaving its custody. Thus in honoring your banner they honor you. To-day a duplicate of it waves over this impressive scene.

The dedication of the National Cemetery here took place November, 1863, and after an eloquent oration by the Hon. Edward Everett, Abraham Lincoln, then President of these United States, spoke as follows: "Four-score and seven years ago our fathers brought forth on this continent a new Nation, conceived in liberty, and dedicated to the proposition that all men are created equal. Now we are engaged in a great Civil War, testing whether that Nation, or any nation so conceived and so dedicated, can long endure. We are met on a great battle-field of that war. We have come to dedicate a portion of that field as a final resting-place for those who here gave their lives that that Nation might live. It is altogether fitting and proper that we should do this. But in a larger sense we cannot dedicate, we cannot consecrate, we cannot hallow this ground. The brave men, living and dead, who struggled here, have consecrated it far above our poor power to add or detract. The world will little note, nor long remember, what we say here, but it can never forget what they did here. It is for us, the living, rather to be dedicated here to the unfinished work which they who fought here have thus far nobly advanced. It is rather for us to be here dedicated to the great task remaining before us—that from these honored dead we take increased devotion to that cause for which they gave the last full measure of devotion—that we here highly resolve that these dead shall not have died in vain—that this Nation, under God, shall have a new birth of freedom—and that government of the people, by the people, for the people, shall not perish from the earth."

For me to add to these immortal words would be presumptuous, but I can urge all true patriots to treasure up in their hearts the noble sentiments contained therein.

The Hon. John M. Farquhar, M. C., our Representative from this district, was then introduced, and delivered an eloquent and impressive address, in which he argued that the cause of the war, as advocated by the South, was not tenable: that capital owning the labor, that is human slavery, which was in fact the foundation of the Rebellion, was the most complete example of such ownership — thus tarnishing the fame of all who fought for its retention. That the perpetuity of this Union remains, and those who hold the proposition, that each man has freedom in the sense of equality, only is a friend of this Union. Major Farquhar dwelt upon the heroic work accomplished by the Battery during its period of enlistment, especially that action of July 2, 1863, the scene of the repulse of the "Tigers," being the spot marked by the monument now being dedicated. That notwithstanding the fact that he was a soldier in this war, yet he would claim it as a special privilege if he could say that he had belonged to Wiedrich's Battery.

Miss Nettie Wiedrich, daughter of the colonel, was then introduced, and read a short poem entitled "The Heights of Gettysburg," embodying the supposed recitation by a member of the Battery of his experience while there before and during the action. The young woman recited the verses with such grace and expression as drew from the veterans the most hearty applause.

THE HEIGHTS OF GETTYSBURG.

From Chancellorsville to this fair hill,
Where the peaceful dead lie sleeping,
Our Battery came, and we a faithful watch were keeping;
Thus we waited, waited, for the day,
   Upon these heights of Gettysburg.

We heard all day those Rebel guns,
Their roar was never ceasing;
Our brave men faltered not, their tireless step still keeping,
    Upon these heights of Gettysburg.

The evening came, with it our men
Who fought that fight 'gainst odds;
All marching firm and true, on they came
    Near to these heights of Gettysburg.

Now press they on, the dreaded foe;
We saw them take our men, when
Crowding through the narrow street;
    Near to these heights of Gettysburg.

"Steady, my men, be true,"
Our Captain said, with mien that bode
Sure death to those who followed ours
    Up to these heights of Gettysburg.

"Fire!" and then the roar of cannon
Startled the rushing throng;
As shrinking from those shot, they fled
    Far from these heights of Gettysburg.

East and West, to North and South
We held the foe at bay;
Thrice were they driven those fatal days
    From these fair heights of Gettysburg.

      *   *   *   *

And now we here, upon this field,
Renew our patriot vows, and pray
That never more will brethren meet as foes
    On these fair hills of Gettysburg.

Jerome B. Greene, M. D., of Providence, R. I., surgeon of the regiment of artillery to which this Battery was attached, was present, and read the poem entitled "Restoration," which he had written and dedicated to the Battery, as follows:

RESTORATION.

BY JEROME B. GREENE, M. D.

The theme of our dreaming rests in things of the past,
Which float as a vision, like a wisp on the blast.
While visions and fancies like the mist pass away,
These dreams seem more real than the things of to-day.
Loud the bugle was sounding its war-note, to arm;
Then gaily waved banners, with loud cheering and song,
Wild music, rude marching of an armed awkward throng.
Then came the departure, with the hearty good-bye,
Wives, mothers and sweethearts, with a tear-moistened eye;
Long suspense, then the battle, then news of the fray,
Then a year seemed as ages,—seems now but a day.

Now we see on these hillsides the dying and dead,
Strong hearts pressing forward with firm, martial tread,
Through the rifle's sharp rattle roars deep booming gun;
Hear the clash of the sabre, gleaming red in the sun,
Hear whir of the minie and screech of the shell,
See the charge (fatal folly), hear ear-piercing yell;
See the line as it wavers, hear drums' hurried beat,
Hear recall of bugle, see the rout and retreat;
See the bronzed, fearless veterans that led on that day,
Like the mist on the meadow by the wind swept away.

By a brook fringed by willows in the alder's cool shade,
Maimed men, without murmur, felt the surgeon's keen blade.
Will to do, tanned veterans, once ready and strong,
Waiting, fighting misfortune with story and song;
First the truce, then the parole; then in long broken line
Came the train for the wounded through the shaded ravine.
None too soon, thrice welcome was the train on that day,
Still a few silent comrades were not borne away.
With the truce came a detail armed with pickaxe and spade,
Christened "sextons," "grave-diggers," "the shovel brigade."
Beyond on the hillside, there our dead comrades lay,
A few spades of gravel were thrown on their clay.

Where an old comrade entered the woods hedged with vine,
There the foe lay in ambush on strong picket line ;
Now we hear the sharp challenge, "Halt! halt! who goes there?"
No watchword, but the rifle's sharp crack on the air.
Killed, missing, who was he? covered deep in the leaves ;
The gleaner of trophies there shall find in the sheaves
One canteen, a belt-clasp, tarnished buttons a few,
Marked U. S. shreds of clothing tinged with old army blue ;
One rusty Sharp's rifle, with a fragment of lock,
With doubtful initial rudely carved in its stock ;
Leaden ball, jagged and flattened, a buckshot or two,
Crumbling bones, scraps of leather, an old army shoe ;
Knife and fork, old buckles, spoon, a few trifles more,
With Greek cross of metal, signed C. S. Fifth Corps.
Though visions and phantoms like the mist pass away,
Such scenes are as real as the things of to-day.

Where the trumpet-vine twines by the palmetto's shade,
Where the sunlight and shadows with twilight had played,
Where the moccasin glides, where the jessamine blooms,
Where the magnolia casts its sweetest perfumes,
The cardinal's note is the herald of day;
Here the mocking-bird chants his long roundelay,
Here, too, paced the lone picket on his silent beat,
Here, too, rest his ashes in this dreary retreat.
Half hid by the herbage and by moss overgrown,
Here smoulders the ashes of the missing, "Unknown."
But the grass grows the greener, and ranker the vine,
While the long weeping tendrils more tenderly twine ;
The birds sing more sweetly and the wild roses bloom,
The wild grass waves gently as the dead warrior's plume.
Dreams, phantoms and visions like the clouds pass away,
But the grief for the missing lives with things of to-day.

As the waves of the ocean recede but to flow,
So the tide of the conflict would ebb to and fro ;
Here the flood-tide of folly, and valor and pride,
Was stayed and turned backward as drift on the tide ;

The mariner is warned by the surf's surging roar
Of the rocks, of the shoals, by the wrecks on the shore ;
Let the victors and vanquished throughout this broad land
Learn lessons of wisdom from the wrecks on this strand.

Hail! The conflict is over, day of peace dawned at last,
The sunshine seems brighter after storm-clouds have passed.
Through the war-clouds of conflict, disaster or woe,
Now the sunlight of gladness and friendship shall flow ;
Where the moss-covered tablet marks this stained hallowed ground,
Where tall shaft with signet with immortelles are crowned.
Here sons of bronzed veterans, both the Blue and the Gray,
Can sport on these hillsides in the sunshine of May.

The bugle and rifle now hang high on the wall
Where the battle-flags droop from the dust of the hall ;
Now the sword to its scabbard cleaves hard of its rust,
Flag and staff, spurs and saddle must mingle with dust.
As the girdle and bridle, all worn in the fray,
So the war-horse and rider are passing away.
Now the moth-eaten garments, soiled, mouldered and worn,
Sash, signet and gauntlet all are tarnished and torn.
And the plowman deep down in the furrow has turned
The old smouldering embers where camp-fire had burned.
Now the blood of the carnage, on valley and plain,
Paints the tints on the roses and strengthens the grain.
May the grass on these hillsides grow greener to-day,
And the birds sing more sweetly in the sunshine of May.

Shall the gleaner glean grapes of the thistle or thorn?
Shall the tares yield in harvest full rich golden corn?
The deeds of our fathers yielded fruits which we see ;
The seeds we are sowing, showing fruits yet to be.
Now the children to be in the future shall know,
By the fruits which they glean of the seeds which we sow.
Words and deeds of to-day, all well said, all well done,
Are but seeds that the father has sown for the son.
And the dark crimson willows by the brookside to-day
Seem blood-stains of heroes of the Blue and the Gray.

Grant the heart of the South felt its cause to be just,
So the heart of the North was as true to its trust.
Now let hand join in hand that was tried on the field,
Sustain the same ensign, stand firm as its shield.
Let the blade in its scabbard cleave hard of its rust,
Let the moth-eaten garments all moulder in dust.
Rekindle the embers of the old altar fires
Long ago fanned to flame by the breath of our sires.
Turn deep in the furrow envy, malice and fear,
Sing aloud the one anthem, giving cheer upon cheer ;
The conflict is over, chime the bells loud and long,
Keep step to the Union with loud huzza and song ;
Since the soldiers and sailors clasped hands long ago—
In the North and the South they clasped hands long ago—
Sing aloud the grand pæan, the watchword shall be :
One purpose, one country, one flag and 'tis free.

At its conclusion, Dr. Greene was heartily applauded. Col. Wiedrich had prepared the following to present to the representative of the Battle-field Association ; but none being present, this part of the ceremony was omitted, but to preserve it, it is incorporated with the exercises :

To you, sir, as the representative of the State of New York and as a Commissioner in charge of these monuments, which a grateful State has erected, and in behalf of the members of Battery I, First New York Light Artillery, I return you grateful thanks, and now place into your care and keeping this memorial to their memory, and of the occasion which led to its erection. Ever keep it in order, so that the generations to come that visit this spot will ever remember that upon this ground was fought the Battle of Freedom.

This ended the exercises proper, after which Tipton, the photographer, took a view of the members of the Battery and the friends accompanying. After dinner a drive was attempted over the battle-field, between the frequent showers. It proved clear until the party reached the vicinity of Little Round Top, when the flood-gates opened with such impetuosity that instead of going up higher, they came down as gracefully as the circumstances and rough roads would permit.

It was expected that the 73d Pennsylvania Regiment, which supported the Battery upon the left and helped repel the "Tigers," would have their dedication at the time, but that has been postponed until September.

John Kappel of Milwaukee, Wis., George F. Schwartz of South Carolina, former members of the Battery, were also present, accompanied by ther wives.

Col. Wiedrich and daughter, Miss Schmitt, Lieut. Jacob Schenkelberger, Ald. Beck and Mrs. Beck, Mr. and Mrs. Adam Schell, Mr. and Mrs. Henry J. Fox, Mr. and Mrs. W. E. Litz, Miss Bachert, and John Messinger and son left the party at Harrisburg for a few days' sight-seeing in Washington.

This ended a most delightful trip and season of great enjoyment to the surviving veterans, which but for the generosity of the patriot citizens of this city they could not have participated in.

From the Philadelphia *Press*, Tuesday, May 21, 1889:

DEDICATION AT GETTYSBURG — THE SURVIVORS OF WIEDRICH'S NEW YORK BATTERY I MEET ON THE FIELD.

GETTYSBURG, May 20 [Special].—The survivors of Wiedrich's Battery I, First New York Artillery, to-day opened the season of '89 with the dedication of its monument on this battle-field. The party, numbering about fifty, arrived from Buffalo, New York, this morning and proceeded at once to their monument, where the exercises were held. Colonel M. Wiedrich, who commanded the Battery during the fight, presided, and introduced Hon. John M. Farquhar, who delivered the oration. Cyrus K. Remington gave a brief account of the part played by the command during the war.

Two poems were read, one by Miss Nettie Wiedrich, entitled "The Heights of Gettysburg," and one by Surgeon J. B. Greene and dedicated to the Battery.

The monument stands on East Cemetery Hill, some distance north of the observatory, and has one of the finest positions on the field. It is massively built of granite, with the cap-piece surmounted by cannon-balls. In the front of the die is a bronze plate, representing a piece in action, surmounted by the artillerymen. The whole is about twelve feet high and bears suitable inscriptions.

The Battery was engaged in one of the bloodiest charges made during the battle. It was in the center of the Union line which repulsed the "Louisiana Tigers," when they assaulted the hill on the evening of the 2d. The Battery's loss in this assault was three killed and nine wounded.

From the Buffalo *Commercial:*

THE OLD SOLDIERS AT GETTYSBURG.

A dispatch from Gettysburg last night says: Wiedrich's Battery I, First New York Artillery, dedicated its monument here to-day. It is on the summit of East Cemetery Hill close to the observatory and is of granite about twelve feet high. It is massively built and bears on its front a bronze plate of a cannon in action. Balls ornament the corners of the cap-stone.

The exercises were conducted by Colonel Wiedrich. The Hon. John M. Farquhar delivered the oration, Cyrus K. Remington gave a short history of the command, and poems were read by Miss Nettie Wiedrich and Surgeon J. B. Greene.

From the *Sunday Telegram,* Providence, May 26, 1889:

AT GETTYSBURG—DEDICATION OF THE WIEDRICH'S BATTERY SHAFT—A POEM BY DR. J. B. GREENE—THE OLD REDANS STILL STANDING—AN OLD GUNNER.

Dr. Jerome B. Greene of this city read an original poem on the occasion of the dedication of the monument to Battery I, First Regiment New York Light Artillery, at Gettysburg, Pa., last Monday. The poem was retrospective and descriptive, in nine stanzas, and was a vivid word-picture of one of the greatest battles the world has ever known, while the lessons of the terrible strife were touchingly alluded to by the poet. Two of the stanzas are here given :

* * * * * *

Now we see on these hillsides the dying and dead,
Strong hearts pressing forward, with firm, martial tread,
Through the rifle's sharp rattle roars deep booming gun ;
Hear the clash of the sabre, gleaming red in the sun,
Hear whir of the minie and screech of the shell ;
See the charge (fatal folly) hear ear-piercing yell ;
See the line as it wavers, hear drums' hurried beat,
Hear recall of bugle, see the rout and retreat ;
And the dark crimson willows of the brookside to-day,
Seem blood-stains of heroes of the Blue and the Gray.

* * * * * *

Where the trumpet vine twines by the palmetto's shade,
Where the sunlight and shadows with twilight has played,
Where the moccasin glides, where the jessamine blooms,
Where the magnolia casts its sweetest perfumes,
The cardinal's note is the herald of day ;
Here the mocking-bird chants his long roundelay,
Here, too, paced the lone picket on his silent beat,
Here, too, rest his ashes in this dreary retreat,
Half hid by the herbage, and by moss overgrown,
Here smoulders the ashes of the missing, " Unknown."
But the grass grows the greener, and ranker the vine,
While the long weeping tendrils more tenderly twine ;
The birds sing more sweetly and the wild roses bloom,
The wild grass waves gently as the dead warrior's plume.
Dreams, phantoms and visions like the clouds pass away ;
But the grief for the missing lives with things of to-day.

"WIEDRICH'S BATTERY."

Battery I, alluded to above, was generally known as "Wiedrich's Battery," taking its name from its captain, and was one of the fighting batteries of the war. It served through the entire War of the Rebellion, but of its 250 members who went into the field only thirty-five survivors could be mustered last Monday. It was at the second battle of Bull Run, at Lookout Mountain, Gettysburg, Atlanta, and in Sherman's famous March to the Sea. Dr. Greene

BATTLE MONUMENT ON EAST CEMETERY HILL, GETTYSBURG.

Dedicated May 20, 1889.

was connected with it from the early spring of '62 to the winter of '63, and was in all its campaigns up to the battle of Gettysburg, just before which he was commissioned Surgeon of the Fifth Rhode Island Heavy Artillery, and went to North Carolina. Wiedrich's Battery was composed mostly of Germans from Buffalo, the majority of whom were quiet, brave men, like their commander. Among these were Lieut. Schenkelberger and Sergt. Moeller, both of whom were wounded at the second battle of Bull Run, Dr. Greene amputating a leg for the former and an arm for the latter. The lieutenant, now a pension agent, was present at the dedicatory services Monday, but the sergeant is an invalid and was absent.

In the battle of Gettysburg the Union line, Barlow's division, commanded by Gen. Ames, lay along the stone wall at the base of the hill. Wiedrich's Battery was posted behind the redans north of the cross-wall; Stuart's Battery B, Fourth United States, stood towards the cemetery, in the field and road; Rickett's Pennsylvania battery was on the south of the wall, with Reynolds' New York battery still further down the hill. The redans behind which Wiedrich's Battery performed such valiant work, and did not surrender, are still standing to-day, in exactly the same shape as in the battle, except for the heavy growth of green now on their crests and sides. Parrott guns, like those used in the action, are at the redans, and veterans can pick out many precise spots there which to them seems hallowed ground. The monument is to the extreme right of Cemetery Hill, close by the original works. There for three long days the awful tide of battle ebbed and flowed; with clubbed muskets the opposing lines fought at times, and it is reported that of the 1,700 Confederates who charged at this one point only 400 returned.

THE MONUMENT'S DEDICATION.

The dedicatory services at the monument on Monday were begun with an address by Veteran Cyrus K. Remington. Then followed an oration by Congressman Farquhar of the Buffalo, N. Y., district, the poem by Dr. Greene and a poem by Miss Wiedrich, the "daughter of the regiment," who, Dr. Greene says, is as modest and unassuming as her father, and who delivered her poem in tones as clear and harmonious as those uttered by a stray mocking-bird which had ventured as far as Gettysburg, and which warbled in the tree-tops during the recitation by the young lady. Afar off, on hill and valley, could be seen masses of flowers and living green, while the grass on the old battle-field grew tall and rank from the soil which had been enriched by the bodies of thousands of the bravest wearers of the Blue and the Gray.

From the *Courier*:

BUFFALO VETERANS—MEMBERS OF WIEDRICH'S FAMOUS BATTERY AT THE WHITE HOUSE—NOT AFTER OFFICES—THE BRAVE OLD BOYS IN BLUE COMING HOME TO-DAY.

WASHINGTON, May 24 [Special].—A number of the veterans of Wiedrich's Battery, including Col. Wiedrich, have been in Washington during the past twenty-four hours, having come from Gettysburg, where they dedicated the monument recently erected to commemorate the gallant deeds performed by the Battery at the battle there. They were introduced yesterday to the President by Congressman Farquhar, who made a speech on the battle-field during the ceremonies.

Special dispatch to Buffalo *Commercial*:

AT WASHINGTON—A BUFFALO DELEGATION AT THE WHITE HOUSE—THE GETTYSBURG MONUMENT TO THE WIEDRICH'S BATTERY.

WASHINGTON, D. C., May 24.—There was another Buffalo delegation at the White House yesterday afternoon. Congressman Farquhar headed an excursion party, which simply wanted to shake hands with the President. The little crowd has been at Gettysburg, dedicating the monument to the Wiedrich's Battery, the battery that held the key at Gettysburg right alongside of Rickett's. The party consisted of Messrs. Philip Bachert, Adam Schell, Alderman Beck, Henry J. Fox, Edward A. Schusler, William W. Litz and W. P. Gorges; Mrs. Adam Schell, Fox, Beck, Litz and Schmidt, and the Misses Bachert and Wiedrich.

From the *Express*, May 26th:

Not the least interesting of the week's doings was the trip of surviving members of Wiedrich's Battery and their friends to Gettysburg. The party, numbering forty-eight, left Buffalo last Sunday in the rain, traveled all night in the rain, and on Monday held their exercises on the battle-field, also in the rain. But not even the most persistent of showers could dampen their ardor or rob the occasion of its interest. Col. Wiedrich formed his veterans in line near the monument, which stands on East Cemetery Hill, in one of the finest positions upon this portion of the field. Addresses were made by Mr. Cyrus K. Remington and the Hon. John M. Farquhar of this city; and Miss Nettie Wiedrich, the " Daughter of the Battery," read a poem entitled " The Heights of Gettysburg," in which a member of the Battery recites his experience during the great engagement. We may be sure that the veterans present did not fail to show their appreciation of Miss Wiedrich's contribution to the occasion. Dr. Jerome B. Greene of Providence, R. I., surgeon of the regiment to which the Battery belonged, closed the exercises by reading a poem entitled " Restoration."

The monument thus dedicated is a modest shaft of granite twelve feet high, surmounted by cannon-balls, and bearing a bronze tablet representing a gun in action, surrounded by artillerymen and officers.

The occasion was worthy of greater public attention than it received, and those Buffalonians who shared in its observance were most commendably engaged.

It will not do to forget Gettysburg. Yet—only think of it!— the War is a tale that was told, a part of this country's varied background, to millions of the men and women of to-day. How soon those tragic four years, with eight or ten other years scarcely less tragic, have slipped away up the shrinking perspective of time! It was no mere page of history to those who shared in it; nor can the surviving veteran of to-day ever lose his supreme regard for war-time events.

The National Memorial Day is at hand. To the average citizen —who is always a busy man, little inclined to cultivate sentimental memories, and not at all inclined to do so at personal cost to himself—the day does not bring any very ardent emotion, nor is the impulse to share in its observance strong enough to lend much zest to his participation. The Government orders the observance of the day, and the average citizen, perforce, acquiesces. If it were left to him, the 30th of May would soon cease to be a marked day in the calendar.

Happily, it is not left to him. There are yet in the land—and may there be, lo these many years!—enough surviving veterans of the War to guarantee a proper tribute one day each spring to the heroes who sleep.

Happily, too, the schools have made the day their own. That teacher is worthily employed who aims to fill the hearts of his scholars with the full significance of this floral and funereal ceremony. If the teachers do their duty in the teaching of American history, there will be guaranteed to the Nation, as long as it endures, patriotic citizens who will see that the fit observance of Memorial Day shall not be forgotten among the people.

From the *Express:*

THE SURVIVORS GIVE THANKS—THEY ARE GRATEFUL TO ALL WHO AIDED IN MAKING THEIR DEDICATION A SUCCESS.

At a special meeting of the Committee of Arrangements of the survivors of Wiedrich's Battery, held last Friday, the following preamble and resolutions were adopted :

Whereas, the State of New York, by a commission duly appointed to examine and suggest recommendations regarding the perpetuity of the memory of its patriotic sons who fell upon the sanguinary field of Gettysburg in 1863, made report that in their opinion a monument to each separate command or battery in that contest should mark such position, and that an appropriation should be made for suitable tablets ; and

Whereas, Wiedrich's Battery, then known as Battery I, First New York Light Artillery, held an important position upon Cemetery

Hill during the three days' struggle, and a monument under the commission named has been lately erected there, and was dedicated by appropriate ceremonies on Monday, May 20, 1889; therefore be it

Resolved, That the hearty thanks of the members of this Battery are hereby tendered to those patriotic citizens who so generously subscribed to a fund enabling the survivors to attend a reunion at the dedication; and to Alderman August Beck and Mr. Cyrus K. Remington for their efforts in obtaining subscriptions.

Resolved, That their thanks are also tendered the Hon. John M. Farquhar, our representative in Congress, for his patriotic oration upon that occasion; also to Miss Nettie Wiedrich and Dr. J. B. Greene of Providence, R. I., late surgeon of the Battery, for poems; and Mr. Cyrus K. Remington for an address at that time.

Resolved, That our hearty thanks are tendered to the daily press of this city for valuable space given and notices of the movements of the Battery; without these valuable aids the excursion would not have met with the success that it did.

Resolved, That our thanks are duly tendered to Mr. B. P. Fraser, General Traveling Agent of the Northern Central Railway Company, for his attention and care during our trip to Gettysburg; and to Major Long, the official guide of the battle-field, for assiduous attention.

From the *Evening News:*

A relief train is making up at Charleston, S. C., which will be loaded with provisions and clothing for the sufferers by the awful Pennsylvania floods. The train will represent the charity of Charleston and of the town along the railway. That will be an invasion from the South in marked contrast to the one which gathered at Gettysburg, and it will be memorable in the history of the country.

The following is a list of subscribers to the fund for enabling the surviving members of the Battery to attend the dedication of their monument at Gettysburg, May 20, 1889. It is supposed to be correct; however, an omission or two may possibly be discovered:

Morning Express	$25.00
Buffalo Commercial	25.00
Hon. E. G. Spaulding	25.00
August Beck	25.00
Edward H. Hutchinson	25.00
Solomon Scheu, Jr.	25.00
Marcus M. Drake	25.00
John Miller	25.00
Philip Becker	20.00
Henry W. Box	20.00
Alphonse J. Meyer	20.00
Gerhard Lang	20.00
John Greiner	10.00
Charles Greiner	10.00
Cyrus K. Remington	10.00
Pascal P. Pratt	10.00
George Bleistein	10.00
Hodge Brothers	10.00
George Urban, Jr.	10.00
Josiah Letchworth	10.00
Joseph Metz	10.00
Irlbacker & Davis	10.00
Henry Quinn	10.00
George W. Hayward	5.00
Eugene A. Georger	5.00
George Denner	5.00
John Kreitner	5.00
William Summers	5.00
Jacob Stern	5.00
Frank J. Trautmann	5.00
John J. Kennedy	5.00
Joseph Krumholz	5.00
Stephen Reimann	5.00
W. J. Conners	5.00
Charles E. Williams	5.00
John A. Holloway	5.00
Philip Steingoetter	5.00
William H. Albro	5.00
Joseph E. Barnard	5.00
Philip Wurtz	5.00
James F. Crooker	$5.00
William F. Worthington	5.00
Francis J. Kraft	5.00
Henry Moest	5.00
Christian Klinck	5.00
Buffalo Demokrat	5.00
Oliver J. Eggert	5.00
John Schusler Brewing Co.	5.00
Charles A. Orr	5.00
Alexander Martin	5.00
Lautz Bros. & Co.	5.00
George Rochevot	5.00
Henry Breitwieser & Bro.	5.00
William Hengerer	5.00
J. W. Tillinghast	5.00
S. M. Clement	5.00
Norris Morey	5.00
Alfred H. Sendker	5.00
C. & F. Georger	5.00
John Gisel	5.00
Fuchs Bros.	5.00
Wm. F. Wendt	5.00
John Welker	5.00
Gowans & Stover	5.00
George Denner	5.00
John H. Knepper	5.00
H. L. Kreuder	5.00
Thomas M. Shields	5.00
Samuel J. Dark	5.00
John H. Connor	5.00
John Davey	5.00
A. D. McConnell	5.00
Fred Deming	5.00
George E. Mann	5.00
Charles F. Bishop	5.00
Frank M. Giese	5.00
John H. Ludwig	5.00
James S. Murphy	5.00
Michael Callahan	5.00
Thomas F. Crowley	5.00

Oliver A. Jenkins	$5.00	Samuel G. Dorr, M. D.	$1.50
Beyer & Rupprecht	5.00	Peter Mergenhagen	1.50
John A. Barth	5.00	Patrick Carmody	1.00
Peter Eby	3.00	Dingens Bros.	1.00
Adam Rehm	3.00	Joseph Mergenhagen	1.00
John Howell's Sons	3.00	John Beierlein	1.00
Sahlen & Roland	2.00	Frederick Bissinger	1.00
A. Miller	2.00	John Yox	1.00
Thomas McGreevy	2.00	B. B.	1.00
J. J. White	2.00	Geo. Schier	1.00
Julius Haas	2.00	Eugene Klein	1.00
Potter & Williams	2.00	William H. Jaeger	1.00
John Schus	2.00	John Moest, Jr.	1.00
Edward G. Becker	2.00	Mackey & Williams	1.00
Andrew Richard	2.00	Leroy S. Oatman	1.00
Conrad Machemer	2.00	Charles P. Hohlstein	1.00
Matthias Storck	2.00	Gleason, Eacker & Co.	1.00
Augustus Spitzmiller	2.00	Rea & Powell	1.00
Robert F. Atkins	2.00	Baker & Crouch	1.00
Peter A. Vogt	2.00	A. E. Makely	1.00
Joseph Timmerman	2.00	James W. Duncan	1.00
Henry Koons	2.00	Batterson & Co	1.00
Herman Storck	2.00	George Dittly	1.00
John Johnson	2.00	Robert Moeller	1.00
Jacob Ginther	2.00	Frank Sippel	.50
Gus. C. Zabel	2.00	J. S.	.50
W. Bowen Moore	2.50	A. B.	.50

At a meeting of the survivors of the Battery held in July, it was on motion resolved to hold a reunion of the members on August 19th proximo. A committee was appointed to complete arrangements, which were as follows:

The reunion to take place at Eagle Park, Grand Island, on the day above named; the members and their families only invited; to take a barge at foot of Mill street, at Black Rock, in the morning and make a trip around Grand Island, stopping at Sour Spring Grove and finally at the destination, with the following programme, which was fully and successfully carried out:

```
OVERTURE...........................BY THE STRING BAND.
ROLL CALL AND ADDRESS OF WELCOME...BY COL. M. WIEDRICH.
ADDRESS............................BY CYRUS K. REMINGTON.
RECITATION.........................BY MISS NETTIE WIEDRICH.
MUSIC..............................BY THE BAND.
```

The following veterans answered to the call:

Col. Michael Wiedrich,	Lieut. Christopher Schmitt,
Lieut. Jacob Schenkelberger,	Adam Schell,
Philip Bachert,	Jacob Hehr,
John Stortz,	Cirach Diebold,
Henry Füerschbach,	Chas. Buchleiter,
Christ Horni,	Philip Strang,
Francis Herrmann,	Philip Stemler,
John Messinger,	William Braun,
Frederick Smith,	Jacob Schmitt,
Andrew Seibold.	William I. Moeller.

The following are the names of the absent members, making the total, as known, forty-five:

Diedrich Erdman,	John Garbe,
Henry Klee,	Jacob Hirt,
Nicholas Mangold,	Matt Keller,
Anton Zimmer,	Louis Strang,
George Baer,	George F. Schwartz,
John Zuber,	George Schreier,
Nicholas Stahl,	John Kappel,
Louis Vetter,	George Fischer,
Wellington Miner,	George Burckhard,
George Knorr,	Samuel H. Booth,
John Horn,	Peter Brandel,
John Schneider,	Jacob Seibold,
Martin Schmitt,	Adam Seifert.

Joseph Lichtenberger was with the Battery at the dedication of the monument at Gettysburg; but has since died.

Col. Wiedrich having formed the veterans, in a few and fitting words addressed them and welcomed all to a first reunion; and invited all the friends accompanying to partake of refreshments after the exercises. After which he introduced the speaker, Cyrus K. Remington, who delivered the following address:

FRIENDS AND COMRADES:

The Committee of Arrangements of this Reunion of Company I, First New York Light Artillery, which was generally known during the late Civil War as Wiedrich's Battery, have requested me to make a short address upon the occasion; and the most appropriate subject for me to speak upon is, I think, that of Patriotism.

Implanted in every breast, no matter where the country, state of its civilization or progress in arts or sciences, all who are to the manner born, cherish a warm affection for the home of their childhood; and, if perchance, separated from that home, at the first opportunity take the advantage offered to return and view again those scenes, recounting to others facts so dear to their childhood and the loves of their early days.

You who have borne the burden in protecting and upholding the honor of your native—or, it may be, your adopted—country in her hour of danger, doing noble service in this or other States of this Union, and having revisited some of those stubbornly contested fields, now assemble near the place where your Battery was organized twenty-nine years ago, to recount those trials to us, with the happy assurance that the Union is safe and prosperous; and at the same time to show your children, and your children's children, the benefits they are receiving from your efforts, which under God's protection you have secured for them. None but a soldier knows or can appreciate the difficulties encountered by you during those years of service; yet I am forced to say that many who now reap these inestimable privileges gained by your valor, are among those who begrudge the pittance due for disability. It must also be said, and which I believe to be a fact, that no true soldier has ever consented to receive this stipend as a gift, or to make a false claim for disability upon that government which he so readily stood forth to sustain during those dark days of 1861; for what compensation is two, four, or even eight dollars per month to a man who at that time left a good business or situation, with ordinarily fair prospects, in order to serve his country and to become, by the fatigues incident to that war, so disabled as to be almost if not entirely incapacitated for manual labor thereafter? No; to an honest soldier the pittance is too small; to a dishonest one or a bounty-jumper too large; and from the latter and his abettors it should be entirely withheld. And while speaking of pensions, I will say that I am in favor of granting pensions only to those who are in any manner disabled during the war or from its effects. The reckless manner of granting pensions, especially to men who came from the army in good health, but who had a very good *hospital record*, is not justice to the true and modest men who, if wounded slightly, would rather conceal their injuries than to obtain such a record. To an honorably wounded and disabled soldier a pension cannot be too large.

Washington, in his farewell address, among other important advice, warns us as a people "to beware of foreign entangling alliances;" and to this time we have followed his advice. But although a free and independent people, without such alliances with other nations, yet we are apt to imitate some of their foolish fancies. When we shall have become *thoroughly American* it will be a happy day for this country. All are true Americans who swear allegiance to the Stars and Stripes, born here or in foreign countries.

In the war of the Revolution many of the prominent commanders were from the countries of the Old World. Having fought there the battles of freedom—in many instances, it is true, without success—but being imbued thoroughly with its principles, they offered to this young nation themselves and their swords in her struggle against despotism. They served well, and peace was accorded; and after, when war had again become necessary, their descendants aided us in the contest of 1812; and still a generation later, helping a sister republic in her distress—and successfully, for she is to-day one of the most southern, largest and richest States of our Union.

Now we approach a period within our memory.

When the Southern portion of these United States saw fit to attempt a separation, then it was that the echoes of those guns which were turned against this government upon Major Robert

Anderson's command at Fort Sumter by the State of South Carolina—like the shot which, at Concord in 1775, "was heard around the world,"—echoed through this country from the Atlantic to the Pacific, startling the people as does the lightning from the clouds, and which for a period apparently dies away; but as the thunder which follows awakened the people to a realizing sense of insecurity, and to the fact of the determination of the South to sever, if possible, the bonds uniting them to the North.

Loyalty was not confined to the native-born Americans; for the German element, with other nationalities, vied with each other in offering their services to uphold the government.

At this time the Battery connected with the Sixty-fifth Regiment, N. Y. S. M., was under the command of Captain Michael Wiedrich, and, by a resolution, offered, on the 18th day of January, 1861, their services to the Government of this State. This was accepted on the 21st, three days later; and although they were not then called upon, later they were, under another designation, and noble was the duty performed. This tender was seventy eight days previous to President Lincoln's call for 75,000 volunteers.

The time allotted me will not suffice to dwell upon the record of the Battery, only to say that the volunteering, mustering in and departure for the seat of war, was in every respect a credit to all; and in those battles in which it participated it made itself a name for stubborn valor.

Will you ever forget those desperate conflicts and minor skirmishes in which you were engaged, during those years from Cross Keys to the surrender of Johnston at Raleigh? These names are not yet inscribed upon your colors, but are upon the roll of fame; and in the near future, the pages of history that are to be written will have your records engraved upon them as in letters of gold, which will shine forth to posterity as stars of the first magnitude.

I wish to mention one incident at the battle of Gettysburg, relating particularly to this Battery.

Gen. Ewell of the Confederates was stationed near Rock Creek, upon the eastern line of the battle-field, near and opposite to East Cemetery Hill, upon which was planted Wiedrich's Battery. Ewell had been waiting for some time for the sound of Longstreet's guns as a signal of attack, and it was not until 5 P. M. that the signal came to him, when he immediately opened six batteries from Benner's Hill as a support to Johnson's attack upon Culp's Hill, which is a little to the east of Cemetery Hill; but after an hour's firing these guns were silenced by the Federals. Finding an attempt impossible on the north and northeast sides of Culp's Hill, Johnson determined to attack the Federals in the very gorges of Rock Creek. At half-past six o'clock he opens fire, and now the battle is in progress along the front of both armies.

While Johnson was thus pushing the right of the line on Culp's Hill, those who were defending East Cemetery Hill were about to face one of the historic charges of that famous three days' fight, namely, that of the "Louisiana Tigers."

Just as the sun was disappearing in the west, and while the soft and delicate shadows of twilight were gathering and gently covering the hostile armies, the sentinels upon Cemetery Hill beheld emerging from a valley a dark line of infantry formed for assault; and while those who beheld wondered and waited to see what its meaning was, this mass of infantry moved steadily upward. On it comes with the precision of veterans. Nearer it approaches, and through the fast disappearing daylight are distinguished the veterans of Hoke's and Hay's division—all led by a brigade that never until this hour had known or acknowledged defeat; as the regiments composing the "Tigers" had made themselves such a name that but its mention spread terror, and whenever they had been called upon for a charge, conquered. But the moment they came within range of our riflemen and artillery, they tasted of that death which they so often had made others to feel. The batteries of Wiedrich, Ricketts and Stevens, with infantry of Steinwehr's division, opened upon them with vengeance, and the slaughter was terrific. With Wiedrich and Ricketts fronting them, and Stevens' enfilading fire plowing their ranks—through all this terrible reality they pressed steadily on. The mass of infantry at the lower stone wall, and Howard's upon the heights, poured into their ranks leaden messengers of death. Decimated as were now their numbers, it would never do to retreat—death was preferable; so on they come, bounding as veritable tigers for their prey; but they meet a foe worthy of their steel. They leaped upon and over Wiedrich's guns, until Federals and Confederates were so inextricably mingled that

Stevens was obliged to cease firing for fear of killing friends, while Wiedrich's were forced from their guns by overwhelming numbers. At this juncture they reached the first gun on the left of Ricketts' battery, where the scene is one of intense interest ; for Ricketts pours into their ranks his canister, and by the incessant working of his remaining guns checks in a degree the onward movement of the enemy, until the arrival of Carroll's brigade and of Pennsylvania infantry. With this support, Wiedrich's men rallying, with ramrods, sponge-staffs, and rocks from the adjacent wall, repulse the now thoroughly disheartened "Tigers"—now only so in name—and who, driven back and down the hill, disappear in the darkness, being heard of no more in history as a separate command ; leaving upon that hill nearly a thousand of their number.

One year ago the 20th of May last, through the kindness of friends, to whom we here return grateful thanks, the surviving members of the Battery were enabled to revisit that famous battle-field in order to dedicate, upon the spot where the Battery was posted during those memorable days, a monument generously donated by the State of New York to the memory of her gallant sons.

> The roll of glory ! all for country fell ;
> Their country's favorites, the nation's pride as well ;
> Untitled ye, the brave of veteran rank and file,
> Your fame is lasting as is Egypt's Nile.
>
> You fought the battles, you the victory gained ;
> Knowing your rights, these sacred rights maintain ;
> Your grateful country shall revere your deeds,
> And for the fallen wear eternal weeds.

Gen. Howard, in an official report of the battle of Gettysburg, thus speaks of the battery July 1st : "One battery of the enemy, a little more than a mile north of the cemetery, near the Harrisburg road, could be distinctly seen, and as I had a battery of 3-inch rifled guns, under Wiedrich, near my position, I directed him to fire. He did so, but his shells for the most part fell short. The reason of this irregularity was the poor quality of the ammunition there used. Subsequently these guns did most excellent service." Again: "At 4.30 P. M the columns reached Cemetery Hill, the enemy pressing hard, and made a single attempt to turn our right, ascending the slope northeast of Gettysburg, but his line was instantly broken by Wiedrich's Battery, in position on the heights." In speaking of the assault by the "Tigers," he says: "At Wiedrich's Battery, Gen. Ames, by extraordinary exertions, averted a panic, and the artillerymen, with sponge-staffs and bayonets, forced the enemy back .... This furious onset was met and withstood at every point and lasted less than an hour. .... Were I to accord praise to individuals, I would hardly know where to begin or where to end. .... Also Major Osborn, commanding the artillery, and his battery commanders, and commend them for bravery, faithfulness and efficiency in the discharge of duty."

Gen. Von Steinwehr says: "About 9 P. M. the Louisiana Brigade ('Tigers') made a vigorous charge on the First Brigade of my division, and Wiedrich's Battery, Col. Coster's brigade, and particularly the Twenty-seventh Regiment of Pennsylvania Volunteers, repulsed them. Some succeeded in reaching Wiedrich's Battery, but were driven back by the cannoneers themselves."

Maj. T. W. Osborn, commanding the artillery of the Eleventh Corps, says: "Between 7 and 8 o'clock in the evening a rebel brigade charged from the town upon the hill and upon Capt. Wiedrich's Battery. The charge was very impetuous and the infantry at first gave way and the Battery was held for a moment by the enemy, when the cannoneers rallied with the infantry and, seizing upon any weapons they could reach, threw themselves upon the enemy and assisted to drive them back."

Now notice the modesty of the report of your captain. In his official report he says; "About 8 P. M. the enemy charged on the Battery with a brigade of infantry, which succeeded in turning our infantry, and got into the intrenchments of my Battery. After they were repulsed by our forces I opened on them again with canister with good effect. .... I am happy to say that all the officers and men behaved well and with a determination not to be excelled."

Would any one imagine that this was the official report of the repulse of one of the most desperate and historic charges of the war? Such was the modesty of the Battery all through the campaign.

Let me quote the editorial of the *Express* of May 20, 1889, the day upon which the Battery dedicated their monument at Gettysburg. It seems the most fitting tribute to the Battery that has come under my notice.

"Where Once They Stood.

"More than a quarter of a century ago a stalwart body of brave young men left Buffalo for the fair Southern country. They were going where the sweetness of summer is not cut short by the rigorous winter of our lake country, and where sunshine and flowers and the warmth of the generous South offer a genial welcome to the visitor from the colder North. But little thought those young Buffalonians of such things. Their errand was a dreadful one. They went to spread fire and blood through that fair region. They went to serve grape and canister and shell and solid shot to the brazen dogs of war that growled and howled and roared all through four years of fratricidal strife. They went, not because they loved to see humanity mangled by shrieking missiles, or to witness the burning of homes and the desolation of the land, but because from that Southern country had come tidings that the flag which stands for all we hold dear in America had fallen before the cannon of those who were sworn to uphold and protect it. And though many of that particular group of young men were born under a foreign standard, there rushed not to the front in those dark days any more patriotic little band of Americans than those who formed Wiedrich's Battery.

"The sons of many of those men are older to-day than their fathers were then. The years that dragged so heavily by during that momentous struggle have sprung forward since with everhastening steps. History has been made at lightning speed, and with strong, bold strokes. But nowhere upon its scroll is carved a more worthy roster or a fairer record than that of Wiedrich's Battery. And thirty-two bent, grizzled and wrinkled men marched away from Buffalo yesterday—the remnant of that noble corps—to find once more the spot where their gallant battery stood during the awful three days at Gettysburg, and to mark it, that it may not be forgotten when they are gone. Perchance, too, the old men of Wiedrich's Battery shall find the names of well-loved comrades marking certain lowly green tents in that quiet hillside camp where an august host sleeps in undisturbed peace, awaiting the only reveille that can awaken them. And, if so, they will not be forgotten when their surviving comrades—only thirty-two of them—gather where once all stood together and served their smoking guns.

"Nor will Buffalo forget them. Our city has many memorials on that field. Her sons sleep there. They went from home at various times and in different commands. But, so long as "the mystic chords of memory" stretch from battle-field to hearth, the Buffalo dead at Gettysburg will never be forgotten."

The total enlistments of the Battery were 305 ; of these 12 were killed and missing, 58 died, 58 discharged for disability, 11 transferred to the Invalid Corps, 18 (I am sorry to say) deserted, and 148 were honorably mustered out in 1865, and of these Col. Wiedrich informs me that only 45 men are all that can now be located. Of this remnant only 20 meet to-day for your first annual reunion, and it is indeed a great privilege granted me to-day to have the honor to address you upon the occasion. May you all live to keep many of them, and when the time arrives for you to put off this mortality may you all reap the reward of just and good men.

It may be urged by some that now the Civil War is over that these reunions and recounting of heroic deeds should cease and the matter be forgotten ; but I hold that the only way to keep alive the spark of patriotism in the mind of the nation is in these reunions, and it is to be hoped that the indomitable spirit which possessed our fathers shall descend to us ; for why

> Should familiarity, as has been said,
> Breed contempt for oft-told tales ?
> Our patriotic hearts should never tire
> Of listening to our sire's story—
> Deeds of heroism, crowned with glory.
>
> Though years have sped
> Since all these deeds were done,
> The blessing thro' the father has descended to the son ;
> The fruit of all their toil and pain
> Are now our just and precious gain.
>
> O ye who bask in freedom's light,
> Maintain these gifts so rich and bright
> In all their purity and might ;
> Forget not all thy sires have done
> And keep in trust that guerdon won.

Miss Nettie Wiedrich, daughter of Col. Wiedrich, was then introduced and gave a spirited recitation of the piece entitled "Lookout Mountain," one of the best-known war lyrics of the late George H. Boker, and which was received by the veterans with great enthusiasm. It was, perhaps, the most appropriate piece that could be read, as the Battery fired the first gun in that engagement.

LOOKOUT MOUNTAIN.

"Give me but two brigades," said Hooker, frowning at fortified Lookout,
"And I'll engage to sweep yon mountain clear of that mocking rebel rout!"
At early morning came an order that set the General's face aglow;
"Now," said he to his staff, "draw out my soldiers. Grant says that I may go!"

Hither and thither dash'd each eager colonel to join his regiment,
While a low rumor of the daring purpose ran on from tent to tent;
For the long roll was sounded in the valley, and the keen trumpet's bray,
And the wild laughter of the swarthy veterans, who cried, "We fight to-day!"

The solid tramp of infantry, the rumble of the great jolting gun,
The sharp, clear order, and the fierce steeds neighing, "Why's not the fight begun?"—
All these plain harbingers of sudden conflict broke on the startled ear;
And, last, arose a sound that made your blood leap—the ringing battle cheer.

The lower works were carried at one onset. Like a vast roaring sea
Of lead and fire, our soldiers from the trenches swept out the enemy;
And we could see the gray coats swarming up from the mountain's leafy base,
To join their comrades in the higher fastness—for life or death the race!

Then our long line went winding round the mountain, in a huge serpent track,
And the slant sun upon it flash'd and glimmer'd as on a dragon's back.
Higher and higher the column's head push'd onward, ere the rear moved a man;
And soon the skirmish-lines their straggling volleys and single shots began.

Then the bald head of Lookout flamed and bellowed, and all its batteries woke,
And down the mountain pour'd the bomb-shells, puffing into our eyes the smoke;
And balls and grape-shot rained upon our column, that bore the angry shower
As if it were no more than that soft dropping which scarcely stirs the flower.

Oh, glorious courage that inspires the hero, and runs through all his men!
The heart that fail'd beside the Rappahannock, it was itself again!
The star that circumstance and jealous faction shrouded in envious night,
Here shone with all the splendor of its nature, and with a freer flight!

Hark! hark! there go the well-known crashing volleys, the long-continued roar,
That swells and falls, but never ceases wholly, until the fight is o'er.
Up towards the crystal gates of heaven ascending, the mortal tempest beat,
As if they sought to try their cause together before God's very feet!

We saw our troops had gain'd a footing, almost beneath the topmost ledge,
And back and forth the rival lines went surging upon the dizzy edge.

Sometimes we saw our men fall backward slowly, and groaned in
    our despair ;
Or cheer'd when now and then a stricken rebel plunged out in
    open air,
Down, down, a thousand empty fathoms dropping, his God alone
    knows where !

At eve, thick haze upon the mountain gathered, with rising smoke
    stain'd black,
And not a glimpse of the contending armies shone through the
    swirling rack.
Night fell o'er all ; but still they flash'd their lightnings and roll'd
    their thunders loud,
Though no man knew upon what side was going that battle in
    the cloud.

Night ! what a night ! —of anxious thought and wonder ; but still
    no tidings came
From the bare summit of the trembling mountain, still wrapp'd
    in mist and flame.
But towards the sleepless dawn, stillness, more dreadful than the
    fierce sounds of war,
Settled o'er Nature, as if she stood breathless before the morning
    star.

As the sun rose, dense clouds of smoky vapor boil'd from the
    valley's deeps,
Dragging their torn and ragged edges slowly up through the tree-
    clad steeps,
And rose and rose, till Lookout, like a vision, above us grandly
    stood,
And over his black crags and storm-blanch'd headlands burst the
    warm, golden flood.

Thousands of eyes were fixed upon the mountain, and thousands
    held their breath,
And the vast army, in the valley watching, seem'd touched with
    sudden death.

High o'er us soared great Lookout, robed in purple, a glory on
   his face,
A human meaning in his hard, calm features, beneath that heavenly
   grace.

Out on a crag walk'd something—What? an eagle that treads yon
   giddy height?
Surely no man! But still he clambers forward into the full, rich
   light;
Then up he started, with a sudden motion, and from the blazing
   crag
Flung to the morning breeze and sunny radiance the dear old
   starry flag.

Ah! then what followed? Scarr'd and war-worn soldiers, like
   girls, flush'd thro' their tan,
And down the thousand wrinkles of the battles a thousand tear-
   drops ran;
Men seized each other in return'd embraces, and sobbed for very
   love;
A spirit which made all that moment brothers seem'd falling
   from above.

And, as we gazed, around the mountain's summit our glittering
   files appear'd;
Into the rebel works we saw them marching; and we—we cheer'd,
   we cheer'd!
And they above waved all their flags before us, and join'd our
   frantic shout,
Standing, like demigods, in light and triumph, upon their own
   Lookout!

From the *Express*, August 19th:

The annual reunion of Company I, First Light Artillery, New York State Volunteers, better known as Wiedrich's Battery, will be held at Eagle Park to-day. Addresses will be delivered by Captain Wiedrich, Cyrus K. Remington, and others. Miss Nettie Wiedrich is to recite, and the veterans expect to have a jolly time.

From the *Express*, August 20th:

TWENTY WERE THERE—A SCORE OF MEN WHO FOUGHT WITH WIEDRICH COME TOGETHER.

About one hundred members and friends of Company I, First Light Artillery, New York State Volunteers, better known as Wiedrich's Battery, assembled at Curtiss' boat-house yesterday morning, taking the tug *Matt Wagner* and barge for a trip down the river, stopping at Sour Spring Grove, and also at Eagle Park, the objective point. At this place the reunion exercises were held. They consisted of an address of welcome by Col. Wiedrich, the calling of the roll of veterans (to which only twenty responded), an historical address by Cyrus K. Remington, and the recitation by Miss Nettie Wiedrich of George H. Boker's best-known war lyric, entitled "Lookout Mountain," which was quite appropriate, as this Battery fired the first shot of that battle of the clouds. After these exercises lunch was served, and at 5 P. M. the party left for home, all agreeing that the first reunion was a decided success.

The address of Mr. Remington was able and interesting, and was one of the chief features of the programme. He spoke in highest terms of the patriots of the late war, and recalled some of the many stirring events in its history. He related how Wiedrich's Battery on January 18, 1861, volunteered its services to the Governor of this State, which were accepted three days later; how afterward it had been called upon to do battle for the cause of the Federals, and how it had promptly responded, and entered nobly into the fray, taking gallant part in some of the events most conspicuous in the history of the Civil War. During the course of his remarks Mr. Remington took occasion to quote an editorial which appeared in the *Express* on May 20, 1889, which he designated as the most fitting tribute to the Battery that had ever come under his notice. He recalled the fact that the number of men who had originally composed the Battery was two hundred and ninety-six. Of these, he said, it was reported that forty-five were all that could now be located. In conclusion the speaker expressed himself as proud to have been selected to address the handful of members, who were now assembled upon the occasion of their first annual reunion, and hoped they would live to have many more such events, which he believed were a means of keeping alive the spark of patriotism in the hearts of the nation's citizens.

From the *Courier*, August 20th:

WIEDRICH'S BATTERY SURVIVORS.

The regular annual excursion of the survivors of Wiedrich's Battery was held yesterday in spite of the rain. The members and friends embarked at Curtiss' boat-house, at the foot of Mill street, in the morning and went to Eagle Park, where the exercises were held. The roll-call showed that but twenty veterans were present. A poem, called "Lookout Mountain," was recited by Miss Nettie Wiedrich, and after listening to an historical address by Cyrus K. Remington the party sat down to luncheon. They returned about five o'clock in the afternoon, somewhat damp but still happy.

From the *Evening News*, August 20th:

Only twenty veterans responded to the roll-call of Wiedrich's Battery at the annual reunion yesterday at Eagle Park. Friends swelled the party to one hundred. Cyrus K. Remington's historical address was a very able one.

The Second Annual Reunion of the survivors of the Battery was held on Wednesday, August 26, 1891, at Eagle Park, Grand Island, N. Y., they taking the boat *Vision*, Captain O'Brien, from the foot of Main street at nine o'clock, A. M., accompanied by their families and friends, steamed down the Niagara, touching at Sheenwater and Navy Island, thence to the destination, where an address of welcome was made by Colonel Wiedrich, after which the roll was called, when twenty-one veterans answered as follows:

Colonel Michael Wiedrich,

Lieut. Christopher Schmitt,	Lieut. Jacob Schenkelberger,
Philip Bachert,	Adam Schell,
John Messinger,	John Stortz,
Frederick Smith,	Philip Strang,
Cirach Diebold,	William I. Moeller,
Jacob Hehr,	Philip Stemler,
Charles Horni,	Charles Buchleiter,
William Brown,	Matt Keller,
John Snyder,	A. Seifert,
Henry Fuerschback,	Jacob Schmitt.

Peter Kehl died since last reunion.

The assembly was then addressed by Major the Hon. John M. Farquhar with one of his admirable patriotic speeches, which was listened to with great interest, and at the close was given a rousing approval; after which the veterans adjourned to the grove, where they enjoyed themselves during the afternoon. At 5 P. M. the party returned to the city, all agreeing that these reunions were very enjoyable affairs.

The following, taken from the diary kept by Sergeant Frederick Smith, will be found interesting:

September 24, 1863.—We left Catlett's Station, Va. (where we had been camped since returning from Gettysburg), and marched to Washington, where we arrived the 26th, and loaded our battery on flat cars and left the same evening for the West on the Baltimore & Ohio Railroad and passed through Bellair, O., Columbus, O., Xenia, O., Dayton, O., Richmond, Ind., Indianapolis, Ind., arriving at Louisville, Ky., on the 4th of October. Were well treated along the route by the citizens of the different towns through which we passed and stopped, particularly at Xenia, O., and Richmond, Ind. At the latter place the citizens were called upon by the Mayor to provide for us, as we had no rations with us, and they responded handsomely. In passing through Louisville one of the limbers exploded in one of the principal streets of the city, killing John Fix, the corporal of the piece.

October 5th.—We arrived at Nashville, Tenn. An incident of our stay here was when a detail was made from the Battery to go to the corral, on the outskirts of the city, to get the mules for our baggage train. We went out early in the morning and the negroes at the corral hitched up the mules to the wagons with considerable cursing and clubbing and we were ready to start for camp (which was about two miles) with four men to each wagon, one to drive and the other three to lead, one to each pair of mules, there being six mules to each wagon. But as the mules had never been broke in you can imagine the trouble it was to drive them. Some would back up, others would lie down, and sometimes the six mules in a team would get so tangled up in the harness that it would take an hour to get them in shape again. We finally got into camp when it was pitch dark, and we had orders to unhitch and unharness the mules and tie them up securely ; but instead we left them just as we brought them, not wishing to be kicked to death by a mule in trying to unhitch him. The consequence was the next day the city was running full of stray mules.

October 12th.—We left Nashville and passed through La Vergne, Murfreesboro, Shelbyville, Tallahoma, Cowan's Station, and arrived at a place called Tantallon Station, in the Cumberland Mountains, on the 18th, where we had good times in fishing with hooks made of bent needles, hunting and foraging. On the 2d of November we left here and arrived at Bridgeport, Ala., the same day. We drew new clothing, etc., and left the next day for Lookout Valley, where we arrived on the 5th. During our stay here we were nearly starved. At this time the battles of Missionary Ridge and Lookout Mountain were fought, November 23, 24, 25. The Battery did not take part in the former as a battery. Our horses were nearly all useless from starvation, the few that were fit for duty were sent with their drivers to other batteries in the corps and therefore took part in the battle. We were engaged, however, at the storming of Lookout Mountain on the 24th. During our stay here we were in position on a hill under Lookout Mountain, and the rebels used to shell us every day from the top of Lookout but without doing us any harm further than scattering somebody's dinner to the winds once in a while by a piece of shell flying into the frying pan.

December 20th.—We loaded our guns on a flat-boat and floated down the Tennessee River to Bridgeport, Ala., where we arrived on the 23d, and went into winter quarters and into the cooper business, being employed for several weeks in making staves for clapboarding and shingling a barn about 300 feet long and about 30 feet wide for our horses. Here, also, the men who had served two years or more were given a chance to re-enlist, and a large number took advantage of it, and on the 7th of February, 1864, they left for home on a thirty days' furlough.

March 19th, '64.—We left Bridgeport for Lookout Valley, where we arrived on the 20th. On the 21st our vets returned from their furlough, each of them being well supplied with tin cans and bottles, tobacco, watches, etc., and a good time was had generally as long as the fire-water lasted. During our stay here we were principally occupied in drilling and target practice and fishing in the Tennessee. Lieut. Sahm and Private Armbruster died here. The lieutenant's body was sent home and the private was buried in the valley.

May 4th.—We broke up camp and started on to Atlanta, we having now an entirely new set of officers, only one of whom was a member of the Battery before, i. e., Lieut. Frank Henchen. On this march we camped at Gordon's Mills ; Ringgold, May 5th ; Buzzard's Roost, 7th. Battle here but not engaged.

May 10th.—Left this Roost and arrived at Resaca the 15th and were engaged ; no loss. 16th left the battle-field.

May 20th.—Arrived at or near Cassville.

May 23d.—Left this position and continued march toward Dallas, and were in position for action a great part of the time but did not become engaged, as our infantry drove the Rebs out of their positions without our help.

June 1st.—Marched to the left and took position. (Place unknown to me.)

June 2d.—Fired one round in battery, and up to the 15th were marched from one position to another.

June 16th.—Engaged a Rebel battery in our front. Andrew Klee killed. Left this position and marched toward right flank, one section being with the skirmishers.

June 22d.—At Culp's Farm Gen. Hood advanced on us in two lines of battle. They came out of the woods and had to cross an opening to reach us, but they did not get very far, as our Battery and two other batteries of our corps opened on them with shrapnel or case-shot and drove them back with heavy loss. In this engagement we had no infantry support outside of the skirmishers in our front. Frank Heringer was wounded. (This engagement was illustrated in one of the weeklies, either *Frank Leslie's* or *Harper's Weekly*.)

June 26th.—Marched to right toward Kennesaw Mountain and took position and were engaged ; very heavy artillery and infantry firing here. William Warner killed and H. Fuerschbach and F.

Hubacher wounded. We now continued our march toward the Chattahoochee River, coming into position for action every day but not engaged. The weather very hot.

July 17th.—We crossed the Chattahoochee River, and on the 20th we fought the battle of Peach Tree Creek, which was a very desperate fight, the Rebs making six different charges on our line without gaining their object; 1 killed, 3 wounded.

July 22d.—Rebs retreat and we advance to a position about a mile outside the city of Atlanta under heavy fire from the Rebs, and started to fortify ourselves by building very strong breastworks for our guns and shelling the city at intervals day and night.

July 27th.—Lieut. Frank Henchen was shot in the head by a minie ball and he died about half an hour after.

August 5th.—George Baer was wounded.

August 13th.—Louis Vetter wounded.

August 18th.—John Schell, our blacksmith, was wounded in the foot by a spent shell and died a few days after.

August 25th.—We left the position in front of Atlanta and fell back to the Chattahoochee River.

August 27th.—We crossed the river and went on picket, where we staid until the 2d of September, when we got orders to enter Atlanta, as the Rebels had evacuated. We entered the city the same afternoon. Our corps (20th) was the first to enter. The enemy had destroyed nearly everything to prevent it from falling into our hands. We, however, got considerable tobacco, which was just what we wanted most, next to something to eat. We remained in the city over two months and had a good time attending minstrel shows and dancing parties. Our corps had the material for two minstrel companies and they gave performances every night in two of the city's theatres to crowded houses. Our boys also got well acquainted with some of the Atlanta girls, and one of our number (Philip Cook) being a violinist and another (Val Wagner) an accordeon player, dances were held about twice a week in the houses of some of the girls. When our musicians were not thus engaged they played for stag parties in our own camp.

October 29th.—We received eight months pay. During our stay here the election for President took place, Abraham Lincoln being the Republican candidate and George B. McClellan the Democratic, and those of the boys who were entitled to vote could do so by proxy.

November 15th.—We broke camp and started on the march to the sea and by noon had reached Decatur, Ga., and camped at Stone Mountain at night.

November 16th.—We broke camp and marched till 2 o'clock in the morning, and had hardly got rested when we started off again and marched all day and camped at night.

November 19th.—Passed through Madison, Ga.

November 21st.—Passed through Eatonton, Ga.

November 22d.—We camped at Milledgeville, then the capital of Georgia.

November 24th.—We left Milledgeville and continued the march, sometimes camping at night and sometimes marching all night, passing through Sandersville, Riddleville, Louisville and other small villages, nothing of interest occurring except that the foragers, or "Sherman's Bummers," as they were called, had frequent brushes with the Rebel rear-guard and Rebel bushwhackers. Two of our boys fell into the hands of the bushwhackers on this march, viz., William Hurly and Valentine Wagner, and it is supposed they were killed, as they never returned and were never heard from since. As we had to live on the country it was necessary to send out foragers every day to supply us with rations, and a detail was made for that purpose, but about three-fourths of the members of the Battery went out every day independently and foraged on their own hook. Sometimes we lived like kings, when we passed through a rich district, and at other times like beggars. Nothing escaped the Bummers' keen sight and smell, no matter how and where concealed. Turkeys, chickens, fresh pork, beef, mutton, smoked ham, bacon, sweet potatoes and corn-meal was our principal food. This was about the daily routine until December 9th, when one section of the Battery was ordered into position, the first division of our corps being engaged.

December 10th.—We camped about five miles from Savannah; heavy skirmishing and cannonading on the right.

December 11th.—We marched to the banks of the Savannah River and took position.

December 12th.—We were engaged with a Rebel gunboat and two transports, which came down the river from Augusta. The firing was very hot for about an hour, when the gunboat with one transport retreated up the river, leaving the other transport (*Resolute*) in our possession. No one of the Battery was injured in this engagement, although the Rebs' guns must have been 100-pound rifles, judging from the reports and exploding shells. Nearly all the shots passed over our heads. Some would strike the water in front of us and make a few skips and then pass over us to explode in our rear, where they may have done some execution.

December 20th.—We got orders to take a position at night within about 200 yards from the Rebel line of works, alongside the road leading into the city of Savannah. We were to exchange our guns (10-pounders) for four 32-pounders, Parrott rifles. The Rebels had two 64-pounders, smooth bores, planted behind heavy works in the road, with enough grape and canister piled up around the guns to last them for a day's firing. The ground around there was perfectly flat and thinly wooded by young trees and afforded no protection. The engineers had dug pits for our guns for protection, but how to reach them without noise and attracting the attention of the enemy was a question with us. But as the Battery was always lucky our luck did not forsake us on this occasion, for the Rebels evacuated that night and we entered the city the next day (the 21st), and as we passed through their works we saw then what would have been in store for us in case we would have had to take the position to which we had been ordered. We remained in Savannah till the 17th of January, 1865, nothing of importance happening. On the above date we crossed the Savannah River and camped at Hardeeville, S. C., same night, and the Carolina campaign was begun. We remained at the above camp till the 29th when we started the march again. I have no record of anything now until March 16th when we were engaged all day and also the next day. Do not know the name of the place but it was near Goldsboro, N. C. We arrived there on the 17th and remained till the 10th of March.

April 12th.—Arrived at Raleigh, N. C. Here we heard of Lee's surrender to Gen. Grant and also of the assassination of President Lincoln. While here the Rebel Gen. Johnston surrendered to Gen. W. T. Sherman, but the terms did not suit Gen. Grant, and on the 25th we received marching orders to go for Johnston again, and we marched to a place called Holly Springs. On this march, which took all day, we met large numbers of Johnston's army returning to their homes in squads of ten or fifteen, all going in the opposite direction to us.

April 28th.—We marched back to Raleigh again; had a review before Gen. Grant (who was here now and attended to the surrender of Johnston) and Gen. Sherman.

April 30th.—We left Raleigh for Washington via Richmond. We had only four horses or mules to a gun on this trip instead of six, and sometimes a horse and a mule hitched together.

May 1st.—Crossed Tar River.

May 3d.—Passed through Winsboro.

May 5th.—Crossed Roanoke River.

May 7th.—Crossed Appomattox River.

May 11th.—Passed through Richmond and crossed the James River.

May 12th.—Crossed South Anna and Little Rivers.

May 14th.—Crossed the North Anna.

May 15th.—Passed through the Wilderness and Spottsylvania battle-fields and also passed near Chancellorsville battle-field.

May 16th.—Passed Hartwood Church.

May 24th.—Arrived at Washington for the grand review.

June 2d.—We turned in our guns and equipments at the Arsenal at Washington and on the 6th we left for Buffalo, where we arrived on the morning of the 9th.

P. S.—The last battle in which we were engaged was, I think, at Bentonville, N. C., on the 16th or 17th of March, 1865.

ROSTER

OF

WIEDRICH'S BATTERY.

ROSTER BATTERY 1, FIRST NEW YORK LIGHT ARTILLERY (WIEDRICH'S BATTERY).

Name.	Rank.	Age.	When Joined.	Where Enlisted.	By Whom.	Remarks.
Michael Wiedrich	Captain.	40	Aug. 8, '61,	Buffalo, N. Y.	Capt. Carlin,	Mustered out March 21, '64 to accept Lt.-Col. of 15th New York Heavy Artillery—discharged on account of wounds received in battle of the "Wilderness."
Nicholas Sahm	Lieutenant,	27	Aug. 14, '61,	Lancaster, N. Y.	Capt. Wiedrich,	Wounded in leg at Gettysburg, July '63—promoted to Captain, April 1, '64—died of typhoid dysentery, May 1, '64 at Lookout Mountain, Tenn.
Jacob Schenkelberger.	"		Oct. 18, '61,	Buffalo, N. Y.	"	2d Lieut., Jan. 23, '62—duty defences of Washington till March '62, continues service till wounded in battle 2d Bull Run—leg amputated—discharged Nov. 17, '62 at Washington, D. C.
Diedrich Erdmann	"	37	Aug. 8, '61,	"	"	Resigned September 16, '62.
Christopher Schmitt	Ord'ly Sergt.,	32	Aug. 9, '61,	"	"	Promoted Feb. 10, '62 to 2d Lieut.—promoted Oct. 20, '62 to 1st Lt.—resigned Mar. 15, '64.
Ciarach Diebolt	2d Sergeant,	41	Aug. 24, '61,	"	"	Discharged at Brooks' Station, Va., June 5, '63. for disability.
Peter Kehl	3d "	41	Aug. 26, '61,	"	"	Discharged at Atlanta, Ga., expiration of service.
John Kappel	4th "	29	Aug. 9, '61,	"	"	Wounded in arm at Gettysburg, Pa., July '63—transferred to Invalids' Corps, G. O. War Dept., Nov. 13, '63.
Louis Fickert	5th "	34	Sept. 2, '61,	"	"	Promoted to Sergeant—died at Buffalo, N. Y. Oct. 1, '62.
James Winspear	1st Corporal,	18	Sept. 7, '61,	Lancaster, N. Y.	Lieut. Sahm,	Mustered out at Germantown, Va., Dec. 6, '62 to accept commission.
Valentine Neler	2d "	39	Sept. 13, '61,	Buffalo, N. Y.	Capt. Wiedrich,	Discharged at Fort McHenry, Md., Aug. 29, '62, for disability.
Christoph H. Pfeifer	3d "		Aug. 11, '61,	"	"	Promoted to Sergeant—transferred to Vet. Vols., G. O. 191, '63.
Christian Stock	4th "	18	Sept. 3, '61,	"	"	Promoted to Lieut.—wounded in leg at Gettysburg, July '63—transferred to Co. M, 1st N. Y. Lt. Arty., special order No. 94 from headquarters, April 16, '64.
Jacob Buck	5th "	24	Aug. 24, '61,	"	"	Died at Alexandria, Va., Sept. 19 '62, of wounds received at battle of Freeman's Ford, Va.

Name	Rank	Age	Enlisted	Place	Officer	Remarks
George J. Schaefer	6th Corporal	32	Sept. 3, '61	Buffalo, N. Y.	Capt. Wiedrich	Promoted to Sergt.—reduced Nov. 13, '64—transferred to Vet. Vols., G. O. 191, '63.
Paul Fischer	7th	35	Sept. 23, '61	"	"	Promoted to Sergt.—wounded at Cross Keys, Va., June 8, '62—discharged at Elmira, N. Y., Sept. 30, '64, expiration of service.
John Dietsch	8th	25	Aug. 16, '61	"	"	Promoted to Sergeant, Feb. 10, '65—Vet. Vols. G. O. 191, '63.
Christoph Boller	Bugler	39	Sept. 3, '61	"	"	Transferred to Vet. Vols., G. O. 191, '63.
Samuel Vogel	Harnessmkr.	34	Aug. 23, '61	"	"	Discharged for disability—date unknown.
Frank Hoenig	Farrier	31	Sept. 3, '61	"	"	
John Schell	Blacksmith	35	Aug. 8, '61	"	"	Died near Atlanta, Ga., Aug. 27, '64, of wounds received near Atlanta, broken foot.
Joseph Berger	Wagonmaker		Aug. 17, '61	"	"	Died at Alexandria, Va., Oct. 4, '63.
Andell, Charles	Private	32	Sept. 3, '61	"	S. S. Clapp	Transferred to Vet. Vols., G. O. 191, '63.
Almendinger, Antony	"	31	Mar. 11, '64	"	Capt. Wiedrich	
Armbruster, Francis	"	40	Sept. 12, '61	"	"	Died at Lookout Valley, Tenn., Jan. 18, '64, of typhoid fever.
Arras, Philip	"	38	Oct. 29, '61	Amherst, N. Y.	Lieut. Sahm	Discharged by order of Gen. Blenker at Hunter's Chapel, Va., March 10, '62, for disability.
Adle, Joseph W	"		Sept. 12, '61	Oswego, N. Y.	Lieut. Scott	Promoted to Lieutenant.
Austin, James	"	20	Sept. 2, '61	Buffalo, N. Y.	Capt. Wiedrich	Promoted to Corporal, Feb. 10, '65—Vet. Vols., G. O. 191, '63.
Baer, Jacob	"	35	Sept. 16, '61	"	"	Transferred to Vet. Vols., G. O. 191, '63.
Becker, John	"		Sept. 19, '61	"	"	Discharged for disability—date not known.
Baut, Joseph	"	27	Sept. 2, '61	"	"	Transferred to Vet. Vols., G. O. 191, '63.
Bergmann, Andy	"	30	Sept. 2, '61	"	"	Transferred to Vet. Vols., G. O. 191, '63.
Brandell, Pierre	"	26	Aug. 23, '62	"	Sergt. Fischer	Mustered out with Battery, June 25, '65.
Beecher, Nicholas	"	20	Aug. 19, '62	"	"	Mustered out with Battery, June 25, '65.
Bachert, Jacob	"	19	Aug. 23, '62	"	"	Mustered out with Battery, June 25, '65.
Burgen, Gustav	"	29	Aug. 29, '62	"	"	
Booth, Samuel	"	21	Aug. 16, '62	New York City	Lieut. John	Promoted to Corporal and to Sergeant, transferred to Vet. Vols., G. O. 191, '63.
Bachert, Philip	"	23	Aug. —, '61	Buffalo, N. Y.	Capt. Wiedrich	Promoted to Corporal, Dec. 28, '64—mustered out with Battery, June 25, '65.
Braun, William	"	21	Aug. 18, '62	"	"	Transferred to Vet. Vols., G. O. 191, '63.
Burkhardt, George	"	21	Oct. 18, '61	"	"	
Bolder, Louis	"	31	Sept. 5, '61	"	"	
Barghes, Christian	"	40	Dec. 18, '62	New York City	Lieut. John	Absent, sick, since June 10, '63—place unknown.
Bender, Anton	"	38	Aug. 12, '62	"	"	
Broecht, Gustav	"	21	Aug. 10, '62	"	"	
Brauner, Albert	"	19	Aug. 16, '62	"	"	Wounded at Gettysburg, Pa., July 3, '63.

NAME.	RANK.	AGE.	WHEN JOINED.	WHERE ENLISTED.	BY WHOM.	REMARKS.
Becher, Frank	Private,	35	Mar. 9, '64,	Buffalo, N. Y.	Sergt. H. Day,	Sick since May 4, '64.
Bollig, Henry J.	"	19	Feb. 27, '64,	Clarence, N. Y.	W. F. Rogers,	
Berlinbach, Emanuel	"	36	Nov. 12, '63,	Buffalo, N. Y.	J. Stellwagen,	
Blum, Jacob	"	33	Feb. 26, '64,	"	"	
Baere, George	"	25	Dec. 14, '63,	"	"	Died at Buffalo, N. Y., June 26, '65.
Broombacher, Martin	"	20	Aug. 25, '64,	Rochester, N. Y.	R. Hart,	Died at Strasburg, Va., June 13, '62, of typhoid fever.
Brown, Justus K.	"	36	Sept. 2, '61,	Lancaster, N. Y.	Lieut. Sahm,	Died at Strasburg, Va., June 22, '62, of typhoid fever.
Boehmer, Wolfgang	"	22	Dec. 3, '61,	Buffalo, N. Y.	Lt. Schenkelberger,	Discharged at Ft. McHenry, Md., Aug. 7, '62, for disability.
Buerger, Robert	"	44	Jan. 11, '62,	"	"	Discharged by order of Maj.-Gen. Howard at Stafford C. H., Va., April 15, '63, for disability.
Brack, Jacob	"	25	Nov. 5, '61,	"	"	Promoted to Corporal, Dec. 28, '64.
Buchleiter, Charles	"	32	Aug. 22, '62,	New York City,	Sergt. Fischer,	Discharged with Battery, June 25, '65.
Bergen, Herman	"	20	Dec. 15, '62,	Buffalo, N. Y.	Lieut. John,	Trans. to Invalid's Corps, date of order unknown.
Cook, Philip	"		Aug. 18, '62,	"	Sergt. Fischer,	Deserted at Nashville, Tenn., Sept. 24, '64.
Goethan, Alfred	"	26	Sept. 14, '61,	New York City,	Capt. Wiedrich,	Transferred to Vet. Vols.; G. O. 191, '63.
Cards, Bernhardt	"	19	Nov. 11, '62,	Lancaster, N. Y.	Lieut. John,	Transferred to Vet. Vols.; G. O. 191, '63.
Debel, Joseph	"	21	Sept. 9, '61,	Albany, N. Y.	Lieut. Sahm,	Transferred to Vet. Vols.; G. O. 191, '63.
Deuberich, Herrman	"	37	Nov. 20, '61,	Buffalo, N. Y.	Capt. Wiedrich,	Absent, sick, in hospital from Dec. 18, '64 to April 25, '65.
Derse, John	"	33	Dec. 10, '61,	"	Lt. Schenkelberger,	Absent, sick, at Alexandria, Va.
Dischenger, Jacob	"	35	Aug. 19, '62,	"	Sergt. Fischer,	Absent, sick, in hospital since Sept. 26, '63.
Dufner, Michael	"	19	Aug. 19, '62,	"	Corp'l Smith,	Absent, sick, at New Albany, Ind., since May 4, '64.
Diehl, John F.	"	40	April 27, '63,	New York City,	Lieut. John,	Transferred to Invalid's Corps, Oct. '63.
Doulin, Frederick	"	37	Jan. 3, '63,	"	"	Received commission in the 15th N. Y. Hy. Arty.—date of discharge from Co. unknown.
Dowitsch, Robert	"	26	Aug. 2, '62,	Buffalo, N. Y.	Sergt. Fischer,	Transferred to Vet. Vols., G. O. 191, '65.
Donis, Joseph	"	26	Oct. 8, '62,	"	Lieut. John,	
Engels, Edwald	"	31	Sept. 26, '62,	New York City,	"	
Eifert, Henry	"	34	Dec. 11, '61,	Buffalo, N. Y.	Lt. Schenkelberger,	
Ehm, Otto	"	27	May 2, '63,	New York City,	Lieut. John,	
Ehrle, Frederick	"	27	Nov. 24, '63,	Buffalo, N. Y.	J. Stellwagen,	
Enz, Charles	"	27	July 5, '64,	"	W. F. Rogers,	
Erlich, Adam	"	18	Aug. 25, '64,	Rochester, N. Y.	R. Hart,	
Eberle, Frederick	"		Nov. 30, '62,	New York City,	Lieut. John,	

Name	Rank	Age	Enlisted	Residence	Mustered by	Remarks
Farnholtz, Christoph	Private	40	Aug. 28, '61	Buffalo, N. Y.	Capt. Wiedrich	Transferred to Vet. Vols., G. O. 191, '63.
Fuerschbach, Henry	"	37	Sept. 21, '61	"	"	Wounded at Kennesaw Mountain.
Fliedner, Theodore	"	28	Oct. 24, '62	"	Sergt. Fischer	
Fine, Louis	"	27	Sept. 5, '61	"	Capt. Wiedrich	Died at Harrisonburg, Va., July 24, '62, from wounds received at battle of Cross Keys, Va.
Frank, John	"	44	Nov. 9, '61	"	Lt. Schenkelberger	Discharged at Washington, D. C., Nov. 16, '62, for disability.
Fix, John	"	21	Aug. 23, '62	"	Sergt. Fischer	Died at Louisville, Ky., Oct. 5, '63, by the explosion of a limber.
Fischer, George	"	21	Aug. 23, '61	"	Capt. Wiedrich	Wounded at Bull Run, left wrist—served till '65—transferred to Vet. Vols., G. O. 191, '63.
Feldtmann, Casper	"		Jan. 27, '63	New York City	Lieut. John	Received commission in the 15th N. Y. Hy. Arty., date unknown.
Freeman, George W.	"		Mar. 15, '64	Albany, N. Y.	Gov. State of N. Y.	Promoted to 1st Lieut. on detached service, special order 283, Adj.-Gen. Coffin, Washington, June 6, '65.
Fritzsche, John H	"	21	Feb. 29, '64	Buffalo, N. Y.	W. F. Rogers	Never joined the company.
Geyer, Frederick	"	19	May 5, '63	"	Corp'l Smith	Absent, sick since June 10, '63—place of residence unknown.
Gabel, Jacob	"	22	Aug. 17, '61	Lancaster, N. Y.	Lieut. Sahm	Transferred to Vet. Vols., G. O. 191, '63.
Gieber, Joachim	"	25	Aug. 21, '61	Buffalo, N. Y.	Lt. Schenkelberger	Transferred to Vet. Vols., G. O. 191, '63.
Grundlberger, Conrad	"	29	Jan. 3, '62	"	Sergt. Fischer	Absent, sick since May 22, '64.
Glass, Peter	"	27	Aug. 25, '62	"	Lieut. John	Absent, sick since June 10, '63—place of residence unknown.
Gall, Joseph	"		Sept. 20, '62	New York City		
Grass, John Conrad	"		Mar. 7, '64	Buffalo, N. Y.	W. F. Rogers	Joined company for duty, April 5, '65—no muster or descriptive list.
Goechler, Michael	"	32	Dec. 9, '63	"	J. Stellwagen	
Grosskopf, Julius	"					Deserted at New Haven, Conn., Oct. 20, '63.
Gavater, William	"	25	Sept. 26, '62	New York City	Lieut. John	
Goebel, Gustav	"		Sept. 6, '62	"		
Germain, Philip	"		Oct. 18, '61	Buffalo, N. Y.	Lt. Schenkelberger	Mustered out with Battery, June 25, '65.
Garbe, John	"	20	Sept. 3, '61	Elma, N. Y.	Lieut. Sahm	Promoted to Corporal—struck by spent bullet at Chancellorsville—promoted to Sergeant, Dec. 28, '64—to 1st Sergeant June 12, '65—transferred to Vet. Vols., G. O. 191, '63.
Henchen, Francis	"	20	Sept. 12, '61	Buffalo, N. Y.	Capt. Wiedrich	Promoted to 2d Lieut.—killed in action, Atlanta, Ga., July 27, '64.
Hubacher, Jacob	"	34	Aug. 17, '61	"	"	Transferred to Vet. Vols., G. O. 191, '63—left sick at Savannah, Ga., Jan. 12, '65.

Name.	Rank.	Age.	When Joined.	Where Enlisted.	By Whom.	Remarks.
Hoff, John	Private,	21	Sept. 6, '61,	Buffalo, N. Y.	Capt. Wiedrich,	Transferred to Vet. Vols., G. O. 191, '63.
Herrmann, Francis	"	24	Sept. 21, '61,	"	"	Transferred to Vet. Vols., G. O. 191, '63.
Hartmann, Frank	"	23	Dec. 7, '61,	"	Lt. Schenkelberger,	Transferred to Vet. Vols., G. O. 191, '63.
Haut, Ernst	"	23	Dec. 30, '61,	"	"	Transferred to Vet. Vols., G. O. 191, '63—absent, sick since May 4, '64.
Horn, John	"	36	Aug. 22, '62,	"	Sergt. Fischer,	Mustered out with Battery, June 25, '65.
Herringer, Frank	"	31	Aug. 25, '62,	"	"	Died at New Creek, Va., June 2, '64 of typhoid fever—wounded near Kennesaw Mountain.
Holzschlag, Charles	"	23	Aug. 18, '62,	"	"	Mustered out with Battery, June 25, '65.
Horni, Christian	"	21	Aug. 26, '62,	"	"	Wounded at Gettysburg, July 3, '63.
Hartmann, William	"	32	Sept. 12, '62,	New York City,	Lieut. John,	Sick since June 10, '63—place of res. unknown.
Herzer, Charles	"	22	Sept. 14, '62,	"	"	Left at Raleigh, N. C., April 28, '65.
Hessel, George C	"	22	Nov. 23, '62,	"	"	Commissioned 2d Lieut., 15th Heavy Artillery, May 22, '65.
Hirt, Jacob	"	33	Sept. 23, '61,	"	"	Left sick at Savannah, Ga., Jan. 12, '65.
Heil, Theobald	"	27	Jan. 26, '64,	Buffalo, N. Y.	J. Stellwagen,	Discharged by order of Gen. Rosecrans at Winchester, Va., July 11, '62, for disability.
Hoenes, Henry	"	41	Aug. 10, '61,	"	Capt. Wiedrich,	Discharged at Ft. McHenry, Md., Aug. 30, '62.
Haag, John	"	40	Jan. 18, '62,	"	Lt. Schenkelberger,	Discharged at Alexandria, Va., Feb. 26, '63.
Holz, Alexander	"	28	Aug. 28, '61,	"	Capt. Wiedrich,	Discharged at Indianapolis, Ind.—injured in line of duty Jan. 29, '64.
Hubiz, John	"	27	Aug. 13, '62,	New York City,	Lieut. John,	Died at Chancellorsville, Va., May 6, '63, from wounds received in battle at that place.
Hurley, William	"		Dec. 23, '62,			
Holch, Henry	"	31	Sept. 8, '62,	Buffalo, N. Y.	Sergt. Fischer,	Deserted at Buffalo, N. Y., Sept. 3, '61.
Haller, Frederick	"	29	Aug. 22, '61,	"	Capt. Wiedrich,	Deserted at Buffalo, N. Y., Jan. 4, '62.
Hahn, Sebastian	"	38	Jan. 4, '62,	"	Lt. Schenkelberger,	Deserted at Albany, N. Y., Jan. 21, '62.
Harn, Christian	"	35	Nov. 21, '61,	"	"	Deserted at Buffalo, N. Y., Jan. 3, '62.
Holz, Louis	"	28	Dec. 16, '61,	"	"	
Hart, Philip	"	19	Aug. 23, '62,	"	Sergt. Fischer,	Transferred to V. R. C., date of order unknown.
Hartwicke, Henry	"	21	Aug. 30, '61,	"	Capt. Wiedrich,	Promoted to Corporal, September, '64.
Hehr, Jacob	"	26	Aug. 22, '62,	"	Sergt. Fischer,	Transferred to Vet. Vols., G. O. 191, '63.
Hood, Samuel	"	26	Sept. 3, '61,	"	Lt. Schenkelberger,	
Jourdain, Julius	"	22	Sept. 9, '61,	Lancaster, N. Y.	Lieut. Sahm,	
Jansen, Peter	"		Dec. 18, '62,	New York City,	Lieut. John,	

Name	Rank	Date	Place	Officer	Remarks
Jandison, Theodore	Private			Lt. Schenkelberger,	Discharged at Washington, D. C., Feb. 16, '63, for disability.
Karl, John	"	24 Sept. 4, '61,		Capt. Wiedrich,	Discharged by order of Maj.-Gen. Howard, at Stafford C. H., Va., April 15, '63, for disability.
Kramer, Henry	"	29 Aug. 30, '61,			Transferred to Vet. Vols., G. O. 191, '63.
Klee, Henry	"	30 Oct. 18, '61,		Lt. Schenkelberger,	Transferred to Vet. Vols., G. O. 191, '63.
Kuhn, George	"	29 Aug. 24, '61,		"	Transferred to Vet. Vols., G. O. 191, '63.
Kuemerle, Jacob	"	25 Sept. 3, '61,		Sergt. Fischer,	Transferred to Vet. Vols., G. O. 191, '63.
Klipfel, Jacob	"	18 Aug. 19, '62.			Left sick at Raleigh, N. C., April 21, '65—reported and discharged at Ft. Porter, July 31, '65.
Kehl, John	"	19 Oct. 11, '62,			
Kirchenmeir, Frank	"	39 Jan. 9, '64,		G. A. Scroggs,	
King, Andrew	"	21 Aug. 25, '64,	Rochester, N. Y.	R. Hart,	Mustered out with Battery, June 25, '65.
Kuntz, Albert	"	20 Aug. 25, '64,			
Kern, Philip F.	"	27 Dec. 7, '61,	Buffalo, N. Y.	Lt. Schenkelberger,	Discharged by order of Maj.-Gen. Howard, April 15, '63, for disability.
Kreuser, Louis	"	43 Sept. 5, '61,		Capt. Wiedrich,	Discharged by order of Maj.-Gen. Howard, April 1, '63, for disability.
Kabo, Frederick	"	22 Aug. 26, '61,		"	Discharged at Atlanta, Ga., Sept. 30, '64, expiration of service.
Knorr, George	"	21 Sept. 20, '61,	Lancaster, N. Y.	Lieut. Sahm,	Discharged at Atlanta, Ga., Sept. 30, '64, expiration of service.
Klein, Louis	"	24 Jan. 14, '62,	Buffalo, N. Y.	Lt. Schenkelberger,	Discharged at Cheves House, S. C., Jan. 17, '65, expiration of service.
Klee, Andrew	"	20 Aug. 18, '62,	"	Sergt. Fischer,	Wounded at Chancellorsville—killed in action, June 16, '64, near Marietta, Ga., Culp's Farm.
Knoch, Florian	"	34 Aug. 16, '61,		Capt. Wiedrich,	Died at Freeman's Ford, Va., Aug. 27, '62, from wounds received in that battle.
Knorr, Charles	"	36 Dec. 16, '62,	New York City,	Lieut. John,	Died near Atlanta, Ga., Aug. 7, '64, of chronic diarrhœa.
Kimmel, Jacob	"	37 Sept. 23, '62,	Buffalo, N. Y.	Sergt. Fischer,	Killed in action, July 2, '63, at Gettysburg, Pa.
Kussenberger, Mathias	"	22 Aug. 13, '61,	"	Capt. Wiedrich,	Killed in action, July 2, '63, at Gettysburg, Pa.
Kohl, Charles	"	22 Aug. 9, '61,	"	"	Discharged at Goldsboro, N. C., G. O. War Dept. No. 98, March 26, '65—appointed Hospital Steward, United States Army.
Kenschler, Joseph	"	27 Dec. 23, '62,	New York City,	Lieut. John,	Promoted to Corporal, June 12, '65.
Koch, Xavier	"	29 Feb. 18, '61,	Buffalo, N. Y.	J. Stellwagen,	Mustered out with Battery, June 25, '65.
Keller, Matthew	"	24 Aug. 25, '62,	"	Sergt. Fischer,	Sergt. Fischer,
Kalt, William	"	24 Dec. 27, '62,	New York City,	Lieut. John,	Deserted at Centreville, Va., June 17, '64.
Lortz, Charles	"	25 Sept. 3, '61,	Buffalo, N. Y.	Capt. Wiedrich,	Transferred to Vet. Vols., G. O. 191, '63.
Lieber, William	"	27 Aug. 18, '62,	New York City,	Lieut. John,	

Name.	Rank.	Age.	When Joined.	Where Enlisted.	By Whom.	Remarks.
Lamp, Frederick	Private,		Aug. 13, '62.	New York City.	Lieut. John,	Absent, sick since June 10, '63—place of residence unknown.
Lammert, Frederick	"	34	Mar. 14, '64,	Buffalo, N. Y.	W. H. Topping,	
Lutz, Frederick	"	26	Jan. 20, '64,	"	G. A. Scroggs,	
Loetller, Charles	"	18	Nov. 26, '61,	"	Lt. Schenkelberger,	Died at Winchester, Va., May 24, '62, of typhoid fever.
Lother, George	"	20	Sept. 16, '61,	"	Capt. Wiedrich,	Deserted at Thoroughfare Gap, Va., Nov. 16, '62.
Linneman, Anton	"	22	Oct. 1, '61,	"	"	Discharged at Washington, D. C., Dec. 20, '62, for disability.
Lichtenberger, Joseph	"	36	Aug. 25, '62,	"	Sergt. Fischer,	Discharged at Philadelphia, Pa., Feb. 6, '62, for disability.
Moeller, William	"	32	Sept. 3, '61,	"	Capt. Wiedrich,	Transferred to Vet. Vols., G. O. 191, '63.
Miller, William	"	22	Sept. 3, '61,	"	"	Transferred to Vet. Vols., G. O. 191, '63—mus. out with Battery, June 25, '65.
Martz, Gotfried	"	24	Sept. 3, '61,	"	"	Transferred to Vet. Vols., G. O. 191, '63.
McGibney, Alexander	"	21	Sept. 3, '61,	"	"	Transferred to Vet. Vols., G. O. 191, '63—mus. out with Battery, June 25, '65.
Meyer, John	"	30	Sept. 3, '61,	"	"	Left sick at Goldsboro, N. C., Jan. 14, '65.
Menge, Henry	"	27	Jan. 12, '63,	New York City.	Lieut. John,	
Mufs, Peter	"	39	Aug. 12, '62,	"	"	
Miller, Charles T	"	24	Aug. 17, '64,	Lancaster, N. Y.	W. F. Rogers,	Promoted to Sergeant—Discharged on account of wounds received at 2d battle of Bull Run, Aug. 29, '62—left arm amputated—date of discharge unknown.
Moeller, William I	"	34	Dec. 3, '61,	Buffalo, N. Y.	Lt. Schenkelberger,	Discharged—date unknown.
Mahner, Joseph	"	25	Sept. 2, '61,	"	Capt. Wiedrich,	Discharged at Washington, D. C., Oct. 27, '63, on account of wounds received at Gettysburg, Pa., July 3, '63—arm amputated.
Mathis, Philip	"	39	Oct. 25, '61,	"	Lt. Schenkelberger,	Discharged at Atlanta, Ga., Nov. 11, '64—expiration of service.
Mohr, Henry	"	42	Nov. 12, '61,	"		Transferred to Invalids' Corps, Aug. 28, '63—date of order unknown.
Moeller, August	"	33	Dec. 15, '62,	New York City.	Lieut. John,	Died at Strassburg, Va., June 28, '62 of typhoid fever.
Matz, Blasius	"	27	Aug. 31, '61,	Buffalo, N. Y.	Capt. Wiedrich,	Died at Baltimore, Md., July 11, '62, of typhoid fever.
Muller, Peter C	"	27	Sept. 17, '61,	"	"	

Name	Rank		Date	Residence	Mustered by	Remarks
Metzger, Andrew	Private,	27	Dec. 4, '62,	Buffalo, N. Y.,	Lt. Schenkelberger,	Died in hospital, Oct. 5, '62.
Michael, Frederick	"	33	Sept. 3, '61,	Lancaster, N. Y.	Lieut. Sahm,	Died at Franklin, Va., June 13, '62, while prisoner of war.
McCauley, John C	"	27	Dec. 27, '62,	New York City,	Lieut. John,	Died at Lookout Valley, Tenn., June 24, '64, of typhoid fever.
Michael, Joseph	"	35	Sept. 19, '61,	Buffalo, N. Y.	Capt. Wiedrich,	Deserted at Albany, N. Y., Sept. 8, '62.
Meyer, Joseph	"	24	Jan. 3, '62,	"	Lt. Schenkelberger,	Deserted at Buffalo, N. Y., Jan. 8, '62.
Miller, Anton	"	28	Sept. 3, '61,	"	Capt. Wiedrich,	Transferred to Vet. Vols., G. O. 191, '63.
Miner, Wellington	"	27	Oct. 18, '61,	"	Lt. Schenkelberger,	Discharged May 8, '62, on Surgeon's certificate, on account of wounds received at Malvern Hill
Moessinger, John	"	26	Aug. 20, '62,	"	Sergt. Fischer,	Promoted to Corporal, June 24, '62—mustered out as Sergeant.
May, John	"	24	Sept. 2, '61,	"	Capt. Wiedrich,	Received com. as 2d Lieut.—assigned to "M" Co., 1st N. Y. L. Arty.—Goldsboro, Ga., May 10, '65.
Mangold, Nicholas	"	23	Aug. 25, '62,	"	Sergt. Fischer,	Mustered out with battery, June 25, '65.
Nobe, Henry	"	26	Dec. 22, '62,	"	Capt. Wiedrich,	Absent, sick at Alexandria, Va., since Sept. 23, '63.
Neff, William	"	23	Mar. 7, '64,	"	W. F. Rogers,	
Noll, Ignatz	"	40	Dec. 27, '63,	"	J. Stellwagen,	
Newkirk, Edward	"		Sept. 12, '61,	Oswego, N. Y.	Lieut. Fitzhugh,	Transferred to "M" Co., 1st New York Light Artillery, Oct. 30, '64.
Noyes, George B	"	22	Dec. 6, '62,	New York City,	Lieut. John,	
O'Brian, Michael	"	26	Sept. 9, '61,	Lancaster, N. Y.	Lieut. Sahm,	Discharged at Ward's Mill, Va., May 5, '62, by C. M., for dishonorable conduct.
Oberholz, Henry	"	21	Sept. 21, '61,	Buffalo, N. Y.	Capt. Wiedrich,	Discharged at Fairfax C. H., Va., Oct. 8, '62, for disability.
Paschke, Frank	"	35	Sept. 3, '61,	"	"	Transferred to Vet. Vols., G. O. 191, '63.
Preis, Martin	"	30	Sept. 3, '61,	"	"	Transferred to Vet. Vols., G. O. 191, '63.
Pabst, Alexander	"	38	Dec. 18, '62,	New York City,	Lieut. John,	
Pietermann, John G. E.	"	38	Dec. 15, '63,	Buffalo, N. Y.	L. B. Smith,	
Pflug, Michael	"	18	Mar. 8, '64,	"	W. F. Rogers,	
Pierre, John B	"	45	Aug. 22, '61,	"	Capt. Wiedrich,	Discharged at Fairfax Seminary, Va., for disability.
Plaw, John	"	30	Jan. 3, '62,	"	Lt. Schenkelberger,	Discharged at Washington, D. C., Nov. 20, '62, for disability.
Rohe, Gustav	"	31	Sept. 8, '62,	New York City,	Lieut. John,	
Roller, George	"	32	Nov. 9, '62,	"	"	
Rick, Carl	"	38	Nov. 25, '62,	"	"	
Rosenberg, William	"		Nov. 25, '62,	"	"	
Reitz, Adam	"	19	Nov. 12, '64,	Buffalo, N. Y.	W. H. Topping,	
Runzicher, Oscar	"		Dec. 27, '62,	New York City,	Lieut. John,	Transferred to V. R. C., G. O. 174, War Dept. service '64, April 30, '64.

NAME.	RANK.	AGE.	WHEN JOINED.	WHERE ENLISTED.	BY WHOM.	REMARKS.
Reuss, Conrad	Private,	33	Aug. 28, '62,	New York City,	Lieut. John,	Transferred to V. R. C., order of War Dept., Jan. 10, '65.
Randell, Edward	"	29	Sept. 13, '61,	Buffalo, N. Y.	Capt. Wiedrich,	Deserted at Buffalo, N. Y., Sept. 21, '61.
Seifert, Andrew	"	21	Mar. 1, '64,	"	W. F. Rogers,	Mustered out with battery, June 25, '65.
Schmittberger, Frank	"	38	Mar. 10, '64,	"	"	
Staub, Joseph	"	27	Dec. 12, '63,	"	L. B. Smith,	
Schreier, John	"	38	Feb. 19, '64,	"	J. Stellwagen,	Transferred to Vet. Vols., G. O. 191, '63—left sick at Raleigh, N. C., April 28, '63.
Schaller, Joseph	"	43	Jan. 11, '64,	"	"	
Schell, Vinzenz	"	37	Feb. 19, '64,	"	"	
Schaefer, Christian	"	32	Aug. 13, '61,	"	Capt. Wiedrich,	Discharged—place and date unknown.
Smith, Charles	"	23	Sept. 2, '61,	"	"	Discharged at Ft. McHenry, Md., Sept. 1, '62, for disability.
Smith, Martin	"	38	Aug. 16, '61,	"	"	Discharged at Ft. McHenry, Md., Sept. 1, '62, for disability.
Shirk, George	"	42	Aug. 23, '61,	"	"	
Snearly, Samuel	"	22	Sept. 9, '61,	Lancaster, N. Y.	Lieut. Sahm,	Discharged at Washington, D. C., Sept. 21, '62, for disability.
Schell, Adam	"	26	Aug. 22, '62,	Buffalo, N. Y.	Sergt. Fischer,	Transferred to Invalids' Corps. G. O. 365 War Dept. Service, Nov. 13, '63.
Sorg, Louis	"	18	Sept. 3, '61,	"	"	Transferred to Vet. Vols., G. O. 191, '63.
Sonnenberg, Edward	"	33	Dec. 4, '62,	New York City,	Lieut. John,	Killed in action, July 2, '63, at Gettysburg, Pa.
Schick, Simon	"	23	Mar. 11, '64,	Buffalo, N. Y.	G. H. Stewart,	Killed in action, July 20, '64, at Peach Tree Creek, near Atlanta, Ga.
Schwitzke, Otto	"	33	Aug. 29, '62,	"	Sergt. Fischer,	Killed in action, May 2, '63, at Chancellorsville, Va.
Swanson, Joseph W.	"	29	Aug. 14, '61,	Lancaster, N. Y.	Lieut. Sahm,	
Schmittholz, Joseph Herrman,	"		Dec. 24, '62,	New York City,	Lieut. John,	Deserted at Gettysburg, Pa., July 1, '63.
Schmitt, Alfred	"	30	June 12, '63,	Buffalo, N. Y.	Corp'l Smith,	Never joined the company.
Schmilt, Louis	"	19	April 29, '63,	"	"	Never joined the company.
Stahl, Nicholas	"	34	Sept. 12, '61,	Lancaster, N. Y.	Lieut. Sahm,	Discharged at Atlanta, Ga., Sept. 30, '64—expiration of term of service.
Stemmler, Philip	"	30	Sept. 16, '61,	Buffalo, N. Y.	Capt. Wiedrich,	Discharged at Atlanta, Ga., Sept. 30, '64—expiration of term of service.
Strang, Louis	"	21	Jan. 17, '62,	"	Lt. Schenkelberger,	Discharged at Cheves House, S. C., Jan. 17, '65—expiration of term of service.
Schmitt, George	"	25	Sept. 3, '61,	"	Capt. Wiedrich,	Transferred to Vet. Vols., G. O. 191, '63.
Schwerin, John	"	27	Sept. 3, '61,	"	"	

Name	Rank	Enlisted	Mustered in by	Remarks
Schoen, Christoph	Private	45 Sept. 3, '61, Buffalo, N. Y.	Capt. Wiedrich,	Transferred to Vet. Vols., G. O. 191, '63.
Schwartz, Charles	"	31 Sept. 3, '61, "	"	Transferred to Vet. Vols., G. O. 191, '63.
Schreier, George	"	26 Sept. 3, '61, "	"	Transferred to Vet. Vols., G. O. 191, '63—disch. Dec. 8, '62 at Washington, D. C.
Snearly, William	"	23 Sept. 3, '61, "	"	
Seibold, Jacob	"	39 Sept. 3, '61, "	"	Transferred to Vet. Vols., G. O. 191, '63.
Strang, Philip	"	20 Sept. 3, '61, "	"	Transferred to Vet. Vols., G. O. 191, '63.
Schmitt, Christian	"	41 Aug. 27, '62, "	Sergt. Fischer,	Wounded July 20, '64 at Peach Tree Creek, Ga.
Schoenthal, Christian	"	43 Aug. 19, '62, "	"	
Schlemm, Frederick	"	26 Aug. 26, '62, "	"	Killed at Chancellorsville, May 2, '63.
Schreiber, Mathias	"	18 Aug. 18, '62, "	"	Mustered out with Battery, June 25, '65.
Stortz, John	"	21 Aug. 25, '62, "	"	Mustered out with Battery, June 25, '65.
Smith, Jacob	"	18 Aug. 25, '62, "	"	Mustered out with Battery, June 25, '65.
Schiffler, John M	"	37 Aug. 22, '62, "	"	Taken prisoner, Nov. 20, '64—returned to duty, May 21, '65.
Schneider, John N	"	21 Sept. 30, '62, "	"	
Samson, Charles	"	Dec. 5, '62, New York City,	Lieut. John,	
Schuele, Saveren	"	18, '62, "	"	
Schwartzenbach, Julius	"	Dec. 27, '62, "	"	Absent, sick at Alexandria, Va., since Sept. 23, '63.
Seitz, Louis	"	Dec. 22, '62, "	"	
Stadler, John	"	Aug. 20, '62, "	"	
Steinbach, Frederick	"	23 Sept. 12, '62, Buffalo, N. Y.	Capt. Wiedrich,	Discharged at Columbus, O., April 17, '65, by order of Maj.-Gen. Hooker.
Staudinger, John	"	33 Sept. 21, '62, "	"	
Smith, Philip	"	19 Aug. 19, '62, "	Sergt. Fischer,	Transferred to this Co. and promoted to 1st Lieutenant, Oct. 30, '64—commanding Co. since April 4, '64.
Scot, Warren I	"	26 Dec. 31, '63, Culpepper, Va.	Capt. Wink,	
Schwartz, George F	"	22 Aug. 9, '61, "	Capt. Wiedrich,	Resigned May 26, '63—promoted to 1st Lieut., 15th New York Heavy Artillery.
Smith, Adam M	"	20 Sept. 3, '61, Buffalo, N. Y.	Lieut. John,	Promoted to Sergt.—to Q. M. S., June 12, '65.
Schussler, Theodore	"	Sept. 20, '62, New York City,	Sergt. Fischer,	
Smith, Frederick	"	18 Aug. 18, '62, Buffalo, N. Y.	"	Promoted to Corporal, June 24, '63—to Sergt., June 12, '65.
Springer, Henry	"	39 Sept. 4, '61, "	Capt. Wiedrich,	Discharged at U. S. General Hospital, Baltimore, Md., Oct. 21, '62, for disability.
Taylor, William	"	23 Sept. 3, '61, "	"	Transferred to Vet. Vols., G. O. 191, '63.
Taylor, Enson	"	23 Sept. 3, '61, "	"	Transferred to Vet. Vols., G. O. 191, '63.
Taylor, Armon K	"	18 June 7, '64, Fremont, N. Y.	L. F. Bowen,	
Trede, George	"	Aug. 13, '62, New York City,	Lieut. John,	
Uebelhoer, Philip	"	30 Oct. 9, '61, Buffalo, N. Y.	Lt. Schenkelberger,	Deserted.

Name.	Rank.	Age.	When Joined.	Where Enlisted.	By Whom.	Remarks.
Umerle, Henry	Private,	38	Dec. 4, '62,	New York City,	Lieut. John,	Discharged on order of Surgeon's certificate, May 22, '63.
Ulrich, Charles	"		May 5, '63,	"	"	Transferred to Veteran Vols., G. O. 191, '63—wounded at Savannah, Ga.
Vetter, Louis	"	29	Sept. 3, '61,	Buffalo, N. Y.	Capt. Wiedrich,	Transferred to Vet. Vols., G. O. 191, '63.
Vandebrook, Anton	"	26	Sept. 3, '61,	"	Lieut. John,	Promoted to Corporal, June 24, '63.
Volkner, Arthur	"		Nov. 25, '62,	New York City,	Sergt. Fischer,	Died at Sperryville, Va., Aug. 7, '62, of typhoid fever.
Volk, George	"	23	Aug. 18, '62,	Buffalo, N. Y.	Lieut. Sahm,	
Vandervelde, John	"	21	Aug. 24, '61,	Lancaster, N. Y.		
Voitt, Lawrence	"	38	Jan. 11, '62,	Buffalo, N. Y.	Lt. Schenkelberger,	Deserted at Buffalo, N. Y., Jan. 20, '62.
Vordemeier, Christian	"		Aug. 19, '62,	New York City,	Lieut. John,	
Weller, Jacob	"	18	Aug. 18, '62,	Buffalo, N. Y.	Sergt. Fischer,	Wounded at Gettysburg, July 3, '63—lost an arm—transferred to Invalids' Corps, G. O. 24 War Dept. Service, Jan. 16, '64.
Willig, Jacob	"	31	Nov. 20, '61,	"	Lt. Schenkelberger,	Wounded at Gettysburg, July 3, '63—discharged at Louisville, Ky., Nov. 17, '63, for disability.
Wiedemann, Louis	"	34	Sept. 3, '61,	"	Capt. Wiedrich,	Transferred to Vet. Vols., G. O. 191, '63.
Wilson, Walter	"	23	Sept. 3, '61,	"	"	Transferred to Vet. Vols., G. O. 191, '63.
Weber, Louis	"	21	Aug. 18, '62,	"	Sergt. Fischer,	Mustered out with Battery, June 25, '65.
Wolter, Gottlieb	"	36	Sept. 3, '61,	"	Capt. Wiedrich,	Discharged at Madison, Ind., Oct. 4, '64—expiration of term of service.
Weber, John	"	22	Aug. 18, '62,	"	Sergt. Fischer,	Mustered out with Battery, June 25, '65.
Woodward, James D	"	18	Feb. 23, '64,	"	W. F. Rogers,	
Wagner, Jacob	"	21	May 27, '63,	"	Corp'l Smith,	
Weitze, Henry	"	26	Sept. 3, '61,	"	Capt. Wiedrich,	Transferred to Vet. Vols., G. O. 191, '63.
Wagner, Valentine	"		Aug. 25, '62,	"	Sergt. Fischer,	Killed while foraging in Georgia.
Welle, Edward	"		Oct. 28, '62,	New York City,	Lieut. John,	Died at Chattanooga, Tenn., Sept. 19, '64, of chronic diarrhœa.
Wildies, Albert	"	35	April 22, '63,	Buffalo, "	Corp'l Smith,	Never joined the company.
Walter, Henry	"	42	Aug. 23, '61,	"	Capt. Wiedrich,	Discharged at Cumberland. Md., Aug. 28, '62, for disability.
Winegar, Charles E.	....		Sept. 18, '61,	Lockport, N. Y.	Capt. Cothran,	1st Lieut. Battery "M"—promoted to Captain—transferred to Battery I.
White, Stephen B.	Private,	21	Aug. 28, '61,	"	Lieut. Sahm,	Killed in action, May 2, '63, at Chancellorsville, Va.
Young, Charles	"	19	Mar. 8, '64,	Buffalo, N. Y.	J. A. Dey,	

Zittnan, Peter	Private,	34	Sept. 3, '61, Buffalo, N. Y.	Capt. Wiedrich,	Transferred to Vet. Vols., G. O. 191, '63—left sick at Raleigh, N. C., April 21, '65—reported later at Ft. Porter.
Zimmer, Andrew	"	21	Aug. 23, '62, "	Sergt. Fischer,	Wounded at Gettysburg, Pa., July, '63.
Zimmermann, Felix	"	20	Aug. 21, '62, "	"	
Zimmermann, Albert	"	19	Aug. 19, '62, "	"	Mustered out with Battery, June 25, '65.
Zimmermann, Charles	"	34	Sept. 5, '61, Lancaster, N. Y.	Lieut. Sahm,	Died at Lynchburg, Va., while prisoner of war.
Zimmermann, John	"	44	Nov. 21, '61, Buffalo, N. Y.	Lt. Schenkelberger,	Discharged at Savannah, Ga., Dec. 27, '64—expiration of term of service.
Zann, Peter	"		Aug. 14, '62, New York City,	Lieut. John,	Transferred to Invalids' Corps, G. O. 358, War Dept. Service, Nov. 6, '63.
Zahn, Guenther A	"	44	Sept. 11, '61, Buffalo, N. Y.	Capt. Wiedrich,	Transferred—date and number of order unknown.
Zuber, John	"	20	Aug. 22, '62, "	Sergt. Fischer,	Promoted to Corporal, June 12, '65.

HONORARY MEMBERS.—Elected October 1, 1890 : Ald. AUGUST BECK, Hon. JOHN M. FARQUHAR, CYRUS K. REMINGTON.

APPENDIX.

APPENDIX.

Governor David B. Hill of this State, in his message to the Legislature this year, among other pertinent matters, thus speaks of the action of Congress regarding the National Military Reservation at and near Chattanooga:

EXECUTIVE CHAMBER,
ALBANY, Jan. 6, 1891.

To the Legislature:

The Congress of the United States has provided for purchasing the battle-field of Chickamauga, and obtaining the roads along Missionary Ridge and over Lookout Mountain, and establishing thereon a National Military Park. The State of Georgia has ceded to the United States full jurisdiction over the Chickamauga field, and the authorities of Tennessee have ceded the roads already mentioned.

New York was largely represented on these remote fields in the storming armies which carried Lookout Mountain and Missionary Ridge. Twenty New York organizations took part in these operations.

A National Commission is now engaged in preparing historical tablets to mark all the lines of battle on both fields. The act establishing the park authorizes the States which had troops in these campaigns to erect monuments upon the Government grounds to honor their fighting.

New York has already made most liberal provision for commemorating the deeds of her sons at Gettysburg. I recommend that like action be taken by the State, through the necessary legislation, to preserve the history of New York troops on these celebrated fields about Chattanooga.

As this Battery was closely identified with the battle of Lookout Mountain, the recommendation of Governor Hill is a consummation devoutly to be wished.

The storm of rain that commenced the afternoon the Battery left the city, followed the party to Gettysburg, and terminated in one of the most dreadful floods ever known in Pennsylvania, namely that known as the Johnstown or Conemaugh disaster.

From the *Troy Times:*

WORSE THAN WAR—THE CONEMAUGH FLOOD MORE DESTRUCTIVE THAN MANY GREAT BATTLES.

How great the loss of life in the Conemaugh disaster will never be known. The probability is, however, that it will exceed 10,000. All that can be done is to compare the survivors with the estimated number of people living in the valley before the disaster, which of course will not insure an accurate computation. Furthermore, confusion reigns. Many of the unfortunate inhabitants who lived through that terrible night have left the locality, never to return. An estimate, then, of the living and of the dead is alone possible.

But 10,000 assumed as a near representation of the mortality, who can adequately imagine the full significance of such a destruction? The records of war, of modern war at least, reveal no such slaughter in any single battle. Ten thousand slain implies four and five times that number wounded. Altogether 110,070 Union soldiers were killed during the entire War of the Rebellion; but the loss in the Conemaugh Valley is one-eleventh of that number. Suppose that 200,000 men on both sides laid down their lives on the 2,200 battle-fields of the great contest. There were swept away in one night at the scene of the late disaster more than one-twentieth of the number. The Germans lost 28,274 men in their last struggle with France, the engagements including such terrific conflicts as Gravelotte and Sedan. Yet the total was little, if any, more than double the number of the killed in Johnstown and its vicinity.

But a glance at some special features of this character will more emphatically impress the reader with the extent of the Conemaugh disaster. Gettysburg was the greatest battle of the Civil War. There the Union slain was 3,070, or less than one-third the number of persons who perished in the flood. Add to these figures the loss on the part of the Confederates, and the aggregate is still considerably less than 10,000.

A comparison made with some of the other leading engagements of the war presents a still more marked disparity. At Spottsylvania there were 2,725 Unionists killed; at the Wilderness, 2,246; at Antietam, 2,108; at Cold Harbor, 1,844; at Shiloh, 1,754; at Manassas, 1,747; at Stone's River, 1,730, and at Petersburg, 1,688. If all of these statistics were doubled, in order to approximate to the entire number of killed on these various fields, it would still be easy to see at a glance how far any one of them fell short in mortality of the terrible loss inflicted by the waters of the Conemaugh Valley. Take all of the wreck and agony of any single great conflict like Waterloo or Gettysburg; they cannot compare with the awful destruction and suffering to body and soul involved in the disaster in that Pennsylvania community.

ECHOES OF WAR TIMES—WHY GENERAL SHERMAN WENT TO SAVANNAH INSTEAD OF AUGUSTA.

AUGUSTA, Ga., Aug. 26, 1890.—The question, "Why didn't General Sherman come to Augusta instead of going to Savannah, when he made his great march through Georgia?" has been so often asked and commented upon, and without satisfactory solution, that P. A. Stovall, editor of the *Chronicle*, recently wrote General Sherman on the subject, and now prints the General's reply as follows:

"*My Dear Sir*—The 'march to the sea' from Atlanta was resolved on after Hood had got well on his way to Nashville. I then detached to General Thomas a force sufficient to whip Hood, which he in December, 1864, very handsomely and conclusively did. Still I had left a very respectable army, and resolved to join Grant at Richmond. The distance was one thousand miles, and prudence dictated a change of base at Savannah or Port Royal. Our enemy had garrisons at Macon and Augusta. I figured on both, and passed between to Savannah. Then starting northward, the same problem presented itself in Augusta and Charleston. I figured on both, but passed between. I did not want to drive out their garrisons ahead of me at the crossings of the Santee, Catawba, Pedee, Cape Fear, etc. The moment I passed Columbia the factories, powder mills, and the old stuff accumulated at Augusta were lost to the only two Confederate armies left—Lee's and Hood's. So if you have a military mind you will see I made a better use of Augusta than if I had captured it with all its stores, for which I had no use. I used Augusta twice as a buffer; its garrison was just where it helped me. If the people of Augusta think I slighted them in the winter of 1864-5 by reason of personal friendship formed in 1844, they are mistaken; or if they think I made a mistake in strategy, let them say so, and with the President's consent I think I can send a detachment of 100,000 or so of 'Sherman's Bummers' and their descendants, who will finish up the job without charging Uncle Sam a cent. The truth is, these incidents come back to me in a humorous vein. Of course the Civil War should have ended with Vicksburg and Gettysburg. Every sensible man on earth must have then seen there could be but one result. The leaders of the South took good care not to 'die in the last ditch,' and left brave men like Walker, Adams, Pat Cleburne, etc., to do that.

Yours truly,

W. T. SHERMAN."

Judge John P. Altgeld in the *Forum*, February, 1890:

HOW THE IMMIGRANT SAVED THE NATION.

But for the assistance of the immigrant the election of Abraham Lincoln would have been an impossibility; and had the cry of "America for Americans" prevailed at an earlier period of our history, the nineteenth century would never have seen the great free Republic we see, and the shadow of millions of slaves would to-day darken and curse the continent. The total population of the States in 1860 was 31,183,744, of whom 4,099,152 were foreign born, and of the latter only 216,730 were to be found in all the eleven States which seceded. The remaining States had a total population of

22,313,997, of whom 3,882,122, or a little over one-sixth, were actually foreign born. In every State carried by Lincoln there was a large foreign population, which was mostly, and in some States entirely, Republican, and which continued to be Republican down to a very recent date; and if the vote of this class had been omitted in 1860, it would have reduced Lincoln's vote to such an extent as to defeat him in most of the States which he carried.

It is an indisputable fact that the vote of the naturalized citizen and of his son has been a most powerful and indispensable factor in giving the Republican party the control of the government; and even to-day its power and popularity are greatest in those States in which there is a large naturalized vote. The eleven States which in 1861 hoisted the flag of secession had a population of 8,726,644. Of these only 216,730, or about 2½ per cent., were foreign born, and they were subsequently found to be Unionists.

I do not wish in any manner to belittle the great achievements of the native Americans of the North; I am simply directing attention to the fact that standing alone they could not have elected Lincoln, could not have successfully resisted Southern aggression, and could not have put down the rebellion.

General Henry L. Abbot in the *Forum*, March, 1890:

RECENT PROGRESS IN WAR.

The feeling prevails among us that the knowledge acquired by our veterans in their field service is quite sufficient for the needs of the nation now or in the immediate future. What they do not know about war is supposed to be not worth knowing. But the military world has been moving forward during our twenty-five years of slumber, and such improvements have been made in all kinds of warlike material, that, on a modern battle-field, one of our veterans would feel like a Rip Van Winkle.

SMOKELESS POWDER.

BORDEAUX, Sept. 16, 1890.—At the conclusion of the maneuvers here General Farron, commander of the Eighteenth Army Corps, issued an order of the day, in which he says the use of smokeless powder will make no change in defensive tactics, but will render offensive tactics more difficult. It is, therefore, imperative that commanding officers display great intelligence in choosing position for an attack.

About Equal.

Some statistician has just figured that the total number of people killed and injured on the railroads of the United States during the past year is almost exactly equal to the total loss of killed and wounded Union and Confederate forces at Gettysburg in the War of the Rebellion.

From the Buffalo *Commercial*, May 5, 1890:

Valor and Skill in the Civil War.

Two articles in the May *Century* discuss the relative merits of the Blue and the Gray in the trials of battle. General Theodore A. Dodge writes to the question, "Was either the better soldier?" and Charles A. Patch asks, "Which was the better army?" In conclusion, General Dodge says that his list of fifty battles gives twenty victories to the Confederates, an equal number to the Federals, and leaves ten which may fairly be called drawn. In these fifty battles, at the point of fighting contact, the Confederates outnumbered the Federals by an average of about two per cent.

As regards brilliant assaults upon regular works, the Confederates were never called on to show such devotion as was manifested by the Federals at Fredericksburg, the several assaults at Vicksburg and Port Hudson, Spottsylvania, Cold Harbor and Petersburg. Few trials of fighting qualities, in any war, go beyond some of these.

As will be seen from the table of forces, after the winter of 1863-64 the Union forces so vastly outnumbered the Confederate, that comparison of the merits of actual fighting becomes more difficult. We can deduce little from the battles except stanch purpose on the Federal, and brilliant courage, coupled with marvelously able military management, on the Confederate side. But if one will take the pains to tabulate the numbers actually engaged during all but the last months of the crumbling away of the Confederate armies, there appear plainly two facts: first, that the Confederates, by superior management and better position, opposed to the Federals fully equal numbers at the point of fighting contact;

and secondly, that of the combats during the entire struggle the Federals had their full share of the victories.

It is certain that the statistics of the war rob the wearers of the Blue and the Gray of the right to boast one at the expense of the other. Neither can claim superiority in actual battle. The case bears enough semblance to Greek meeting Greek to satisfy the reasonable aspirations of either " Yank " or " Johnny."

And in this connection it may not be amiss, once more, to give our national self-esteem a *bonne bouche* in the following table :

TABLE OF LOSSES IN SUNDRY BATTLES OF THE EIGHTEENTH AND NINETEENTH CENTURIES.

Percentage of killed and wounded of number engaged.

Prussians—Up to Waterloo, in eight battles	18.42
Prussians—At Königgratz	3.86
Austrians—Up to Waterloo, in seven battles	11.17
Austrians—Since in two	8.56
French—Up to Waterloo, in nine battles	22.38
French—Since in nine	8.86
Germans—Since 1745, in eight battles	11.53
English—In four battles	10.36
Federals—In eleven battles	12.89
Confederates—In eleven battles	14.16

From this table it is manifest that, excepting only the troops of Frederick and of Napoleon, the American volunteer has shown himself equal to taking the severest punishment of any troops upon the field of battle. The wonderfully pertinacious tactics of those two great captains, rather than the discipline of their troops, explains the excess of loss of their battles. And while the capacity to face heavy loss is but one of the elements which go to make up the soldier, it is perhaps of them all the most telling.

Prof. N. S. Shaler in *North American Review*:

AMERICAN HONOR—NO BETRAYAL OF TRUST IN THE CIVIL WAR.

The surprising part of our Civil War—perhaps the most surprising feature in that marvellous contest—was that from the beginning to the end there is no case in which an officer of any grade is known to have gone over to the enemy. Desertions of private soldiers from one side to the other were relatively rare.

There were occasional cases in which men forced into the army on either side took the first chance which offered to range themselves in the army to which their principles attracted them. I have been unable to find a case in which such action was ever taken by any military unit—a company, regiment, or larger corps. Although, under the sting of defeat, a number of our officers of the Federal Army were accused of half-heartedness or treachery, the sober verdict of history has always been in their favor. It was the most satisfactory feature of the Civil War that in the worst mischances of lost battles and unsuccessful campaigns the men never lost their confidence in the moral integrity of their chiefs. Although in the curious freedom of speech which characterized our armies the men frequently condemned their leaders as fools, they never seemed to question the trustworthiness of their motives. I had an opportunity to mingle more or less with soldiers who had suffered a succession of overwhelming defeats, and to hear their camp-fire talk concerning the conditions which led to the disasters they had been compelled to endure. I have heard many expressions of indignation directed against the stupidity of their leaders, but never a suggestion that they were traitors. Most commonly, even in the very extremity of disaster, the tone of criticism was characteristically jocose. The men, as is the good American fashion, took their vengeance in fun. I have heard of the case of a Confederate soldier just captured through the rash conduct of his regimental commander, who, though weeping at the mischance which had befallen him, managed to help himself to a better frame of mind by a characteristic *mot*. He remarked that "that 'ere colonel of ourn was that venturesome, he would walk across hell on a rotten rail for ten cents."

Henry Latchford in the Chicago *Journal*:

LINCOLN AT GETTYSBURG.

Early in the summer of 1875 I was sitting one afternoon beside a barrister friend who was engaged in a chancery suit before one of the English Vice-Chancellors in Lincoln's Inn, London. Some American visitors sat near us, and, in the course of conversation, said that they belonged to Massachusetts, but were anxious to see Judah P. Benjamin, who was to appear in some case during the day.

They were specially interested, because Benjamin was a Jew himself and was engaged to appear against an influential firm of Jewish money lenders. . . . The incident is introduced here as leading up to a discussion about Abraham Lincoln which took place that evening at chambers in the Temple, to which place several lawyers and others had been invited to meet the American visitors. The discussion started on Lincoln early in the evening's proceedings and never wandered away from that subject until we separated in the small hours of the following morning. I remember being struck by what a very scholarly Oxford man said about Lincoln's oration at Gettysburg. He said that at the time it had been delivered Oxford men thought it must have been based upon, or at least suggested by, some one of the ancient Greek orations delivered upon a similar occasion. Accordingly the young men went to their books and, of course, turned up the famous speech, quoted by Socrates for Menexenus, that Aspasia composed and Pericles delivered after a great battle. But Lincoln had evidently not found his inspiration there. Some great funeral orations of antiquity and the Middle Ages were ransacked, but with the same result. "President Lincoln's few words," said the scholar, "formed a nobler utterance than all the recorded funeral orations delivered through the ages."

Gen. Henry L. Abbot in March *Forum:*

The Revolution in Infantry Arms.

In future wars (1) the bullets will have much greater penetrative power, and will therefore be less readily stopped by covering obstacles, whether natural or artificial. (2) The trajectory is flattened; that is, the bullets at decisive battle ranges rise less above the ground, thus not only widening the dangerous space and reducing the number of misses due to a defective estimate of distance, but also extending point-blank range, and thus in a measure doing away with adjustment of the sights under heavy fire. (3) The power of firing a few rounds with excessive rapidity when needful, will make charges more bloody than ever before. Every rush in the close approaches to a position defended even by a thin line of skirmishers, will be met by volleys more intolerable than the heaviest five of a line of battle twenty-five years ago. (4) The reduction in weight of ammunition will enable the soldiers to carry about double the number of rounds, and to receive fresh supplies in action with correspondingly greater ease. (5) The use of smokeless powder will make it more easy to overlook the ground in front, by reason of the absence of the clouds of smoke that heretofore have spread a merciful veil between modern armies in the death struggle ; but, on the other hand, the readiest mode of detecting the precise position of the enemy—his puffs of smoke —will be lacking, and surprises and unexpected movements of skirmishers will probably be more frequent than of old. There will be no longer a curtain to hide the ghastly spectacle immediately around them. Experience has proved that many men who fight steadily in battle, turn faint and sick in a field hospital ; how will it be when the two experiences are to a certain extent combined ?

From the Albany *Journal:*

GENERAL HANCOCK AS A POET.
WRITTEN IN AN AUTOGRAPH ALBUM.

To my Friend:

Wreathe thy garlands, fairest one ;
Ere the beams of day are gone,
Soon will close each fragrant flower
Blooming in the garden's bower,
While the midnight dews are shed
O'er each sleeping flow'ret's head.

Wreathe thy garlands, fairest one ;
Soon will summer's reign be gone,
Tempests come with chilling breath
Sweeping o'er the barren heath
And stern winter's fearless band
Stalk in fierceness o'er the land.

Wreathe thy garlands, fairest one,
Soon will set life's glowing sun,
Youth's gay dreams too quickly fade,
Loving hearts are soon betrayed ;
Wreathe thy garlands ere thy bloom
Fade around thy earthly tomb.

W. S. HANCOCK, December 9, 1839.

From the Chicago *Times:*

The camera will get well down to the front in the next struggle. It will be out on the skirmish line. It will be in the menaced battery. It will take its chances side by side with the colors in the imminent deadly breach. It will move up with the cavalry. Wherever army is hurled at army in the future this sleepless, unforgetting eye will be vigilantly watching, ready to record the truth, ready to carry away the story of heroism or cowardice, of victory or defeat, and to tell it so as to compel conviction.

From the *New York Sun:*

THE SERPENT OF WAR—THEY STRUCK WITH DEADLY EFFECT WHEN THERE WAS NO ENEMY IN SIGHT.

My company lost thirteen men killed and five wounded at the battle of Fair Oaks. If this percentage had been followed out through every company engaged in that battle the total loss would have horrified the world. It wasn't that we lost four or five men in this fight, three or four in that, from two to six in a third, that finally worked a complete metamorphosis in our company and regiment. It was the fangs of the serpent of war; the deadly bite of the dreaded reptile which never rests after the alarm of war has sounded.

We went to the front one hundred and four strong. Before we had even seen a confederate in uniform we had lost seven men. A week after the seventh was buried not one of us could recall how nor where the seven had passed away. The serpent had struck and fever had followed, one had gone insane, one had crept away into a jungle on the Chickahominy and blown out his brains; death had come as surely as if sent from the cannon's mouth, but yet it was insidious. A private soldier in a great army is one of the grains of sand on the seashore. He answers roll call to-night ; to-morrow morning he is not in line. If his absence is remarked it is soon forgotten. He drifts away to the hospital, dies, is buried, his name is dropped from the muster rolls, and in a few weeks he is out of mind.

We lost eleven men between Fair Oaks and Antietam, only one of whom died with uniform on. The other ten were bitten by the unseen serpent of war as they lay on the damp earth, as they drank the waters of the swamps, as they stood guard with the vapor of typhus fever floating around them like smoke. One by one they were marked "absent" at roll call; one by one they drifted out of the whirlpool to die in their beds at Harper's Ferry, Charleston or Washington. Between McClellan at Antietam and Burnside at Fredericksburg the serpent of war struck his poisoned fangs into four more of our men. They had been foremost in the rush upon the guns; they had been first at the enemy's breastworks; they had been praised and complimented for their bravery. The serpent crept among them at midnight, and never an ear heard its movements. He struck them at high noon in the presence of thousands, and never an eye caught sight of his loathsome form. We missed them for a day; hardly longer.

Now and then a man who had been struck did not die. He fled away,—deserted—the victim of sordid melancholy, a soldier whose actions were guided by the vagaries of lunacy. We did not remember him with contempt. Every one of us could feel how it was with him. And others withdrew to the swamps and jungles and there lay down to die alone or to put a sudden end to the sufferings which had become unbearable. We remembered these men with gentleness and sympathy. There were times when each of us had to fight back the same power which they could not resist.

And the serpent crept among us, no matter where we were encamped, and he demanded his victim, no matter who was taken, and so it came about before we sat down in front of Petersburg that our returns read:

```
Killed in action..................................... 24
Wounded and discharged .............................. 17
Deserted ............................................  3
Sick and discharged .................................  7
Bitten by the serpent of war. ....................... 48
```

Thus we had only five men left of the original band, and before the surrender three of these had fallen in action. We had three different captains, two first lieutenants, four second, four first sergeants, and the two sole survivors of the original company, who went out as privates, had shoulder-straps a year before the war closed. After the first year we never numbered over ninety men, and at no time did we ever fall below sixty. Recruits kept coming, but the serpent never rested. The missiles of war would have left us almost half the old company. The fangs of the serpent were less merciful than the heat and turmoil of battle.

On The Death of Lincoln.

O Captain! my Captain! our fearful trip is done;
The ship has weathered every rock, the prize we sought is won;
The port is near, the bells I hear, the people all exulting,
While follow eyes the steady keel, the vessel grim and daring.

> But, O heart! heart! heart!
> O the bleeding drops of red,
> Where on the deck my Captain lies,
> Fallen cold and dead.

O Captain! my Captain! rise up and hear the bells;
Rise up—for you the flag is flung—for you the bugle trills;
For you bouquets and ribbon'd wreaths—for you the shores a-crowding;
For you they call, the swaying mass, their eager faces turning.

> Here, Captain! dear father!
> This arm beneath your head!
> It is some dream that on the deck
> You're fallen cold and dead.

My Captain does not answer, his lips are pale and still;
My father does not feel my arm, he has no pulse nor will;
The ship is anchored safe and sound, its voyage closed and done;
From fearful trip the victor ship comes in with object won.

> Exult, O shores, and ring, O bells!
> But I with mournful tread
> Walk the deck—my Captain lies
> Fallen cold and dead.
>
> —Walt Whitman, 1865.

From the Chicago *Tribune*:

"Smokeless powder" would be death to the battery men. They are accustomed to load their guns under "the cloud of smoke" and drop to the ground before the sharpshooters of the enemy can see to pick them off. The smoke is their protection as every artilleryman can testify. It was said by the Confederates of a celebrated Union battery from Chicago during the war, "It was manned by one man," as never more than one was in sight when the smoke cleared away.

From the *United Service Review*:

A REAL BATTLE — LITTLE OPPORTUNITY FOR DISPLAY OF HEROICS OR POETIC GLORY.

A battle does not consist, as many imagine, in a grand advance of victorious lines of attack, sweeping everything before them, or the helter-skelter flight of the unfortunate defeated. The historian must so present it in his descriptions, the artist in his paintings. Even the writer of an official account must limit himself to the presentation of such moments as demand special treatment, or to such episodes as involve important and instructive tactical movements.

All those events which are less striking, which pass more quietly, but which, nevertheless, contribute to the final result, cannot be reproduced without too much expansion. Those incidents which no account of the battle, official or unofficial, takes any note of— the thousand and one events observed only by the participants, the innumerable cases in which the direction and control of affairs glide out of the hands of the officers—these are the little drops of water that make the mighty ocean of battle and determine victory or defeat.

The opening of the day of a great battle is generally very prosaic. After an uncomfortable night passed in a wet or cold bivouac, where the men, wrapped in their overcoats, have been gathered shivering about the camp-fire, trying in vain to get warm; after the simplest of breakfasts, of which the draught of pure cold water was the only palatable constituent, the soldier goes forth to battle. There he may never even see the enemy; indeed, unusually long halts, uncomfortable standing still under shrapnel fire, or apparently useless camping in mud and under small-arm fire await him. The feeling of being exposed to the invisible missiles of the enemy, mingled with the uncertainty as to what is going on to the right and left, often produces in the best of troops great depression and a consequent falling off in offensive strength, even when the battle in general is making splendid progress. In such moments tactics are exhausted, and it is only a question of grit and sense of duty.

Sheridan tells us: "Indeed, the battle of Chickamauga was something like that of Stone River, victory resting with the side that had the grit to defer longest its relinquishment of the field." Still more pressing is the appeal to the morale of the troops when an unfortunate termination of the battle forces an army which has done its duty to retire. Exhausted to its last gasp, its resistance, pushed to the highest pitch, gives way, and with frightful reaction the resistless mass plunges to the rear. This is to-day no longer an organized retreat from position to position, as our predecessors taught and practiced, but an uncontrollable current, like the mountain torrent, which, fraught with havoc and disaster, overflows its banks. Woe to the land that can oppose no other dams to this stream than strategy, tactics and the instruction of the troops. These will be washed away like sand heaps by the roaring waters.

From the Portland *Telegram:*

HE SAW THE GUNS AT GETTYSBURG.

During the National Encampment in Boston, an old comrade with silvery hair was led into the Cyclorama of Gettysburg by a bright-faced little miss. The old man sat down while the child described to him the features of the picture. Occasionally he asked her a question, and slowly shook his head as if in doubt of the accuracy of her account. She had described to him, in her own way, the on-rush of picket-men and the hand-to-hand conflict at the stone wall, where the Maine Veterans met the charge of the Southerners, when he asked:

"But where's the artillery, May?"

"Oh, you mean the big guns? They're over there on the hill, in a row."

"All in a row?" he asked.

"Yes," she replied.

He shook his head.

"Look around," said he. "There must be some more that are not in line."

"Yes," she said, "there are some more down here, but they are all upset; I guess they're busted."

"Is that where the men are going over the wall?"

"Yes, Grandpa."

"Is there a grove of trees?"

"Yes; it seems to be full of men, but the smoke is so thick you can't see them."

"Oh, I see them," he cried.

It was then noticed by several comrades who were standing near him that he was blind. The little girl replied:

"Oh, no, Grandpa, you can't see them."

"Yes, I can," cried the old soldier; "I can see the men, the grove, and the broken cannon lying about."

The child looked at him in innocent surprise, and said, "You are joking, Grandpa."

"No, my dear," replied the old man. "No. That was the last thing I ever saw on earth. There was a caisson exploded there just this side of the stone wall, and that was the last terrible picture I ever saw, for it was then I lost my eyesight, and I have never got the picture out of my mind."

The foregoing material was ready for the press, when we were greatly pained to learn of the death of General William T. Sherman. Words are inadequate to express our sorrow at the dispensation; and in place of anything we can offer at this time, the following tribute from the *Express* of Sunday, February 15, 1891, happily coincides with our feelings. We also subjoin a historical sketch of the General, from the same source.

WILLIAM TECUMSEH SHERMAN.

Grim and childlike, stern and simple, gruff and warm-hearted. These are the ill-mated words which come to mind at the thought of the great General who passed away so peacefully yesterday afternoon.

Of William Tecumseh Sherman, the warrior, one can judge by the story of his brilliant achievements printed on another page, and by the history of the Civil War, in which his name holds a place scarcely less prominent than that of the other great soldier whom he rejoined yesterday—Ulysses S. Grant. But General Sherman was singularly close-mouthed. He drove the newspaper men from the ranks during the War, and has been on poor terms with them ever since. "He doesn't mean to be discourteous," his distinguished brother once explained. "It's his way. He is as kind-hearted as any man living." So it was that the public knew very little of General Sherman, the man. One or two of his letters, written during the War, tell volumes of his personality

GENERAL SHERMAN'S LIFE—THE STORY OF HIS RISE UNTIL HE BECAME ONE OF THE WORLD'S GREAT GENERALS.

William Tecumseh Sherman was born at Lancaster, O., on February 8, 1820. His father, who was a prominent lawyer and Judge of the Supreme Court of Ohio, died when William was nine years old, leaving a widow with eleven young children, of whom William was the sixth and John the eighth. William was taken into the family of Thomas Ewing, afterward Secretary of the Interior under President Taylor. He was sent to school at Lancaster till he was fifteen years old, when he received an appointment to West Point. He was graduated sixth in a class of forty-two, one of whom was George H. Thomas.

He received his commission as second lieutenant on July 1, 1840, and was assigned to the Third Artillery, doing duty in Florida. The next year he was made a first lieutenant. He served in different parts of the South until the outbreak of the Mexican War in 1846, when he was sent with troops around Cape Horn to California, where he acted as adjutant-general to General Kearney, Colonel Mason, and General Persifer F. Smith. For his services here he was brevetted captain, and on his return to the East he was commissioned a captain in the Commissary Department.

On May 1, 1850, Capt. Sherman married Ellen Boyle Ewing, the daughter of his early benefactor. He resigned from the Army on September 6, 1853, and engaged in banking, representing a St. Louis firm at San Francisco and afterward at New York.

While a lieutenant in 1843 he had begun the study of law in connection with his military duties; and he was now admitted to the bar, and for two years he practiced at Leavenworth, Kansas. In 1859 he was appointed Superintendent of the State Military Academy at Alexandria, La., where he remained until the State seceded from the Union, when he returned to St. Louis.

At the first call for troops Sherman offered his services to the Government. He was commissioned Colonel of the Thirteenth Regular Infantry. General Scott fully appreciated the value of men of Sherman's type. He gave him command of a brigade in Tyler's division of the army that marched to Bull Run and fought that first disastrous battle of the War. Sherman took a prominent part in this battle, and soon after he was commissioned Brigadier-General of Volunteers and sent to Kentucky. For a short time he was in command of the Army of Kentucky. He was succeeded by General Buell.

Just after the capture of Forts Henry and Donelson by General Grant, Sherman was assigned to command a division in the Army of Tennessee. His first distinguished military service was in the battle of Pittsburg Landing and Shiloh, on April 6, 1862. Sherman was in the very thickest of the fight at Shiloh. His division lost

2,034 men. He was himself wounded in the hand in the first day's battle, but he refused to leave the field.

General Grant made special mention of General Sherman in his official report, saying : " To his individual efforts I am indebted for the success of that battle." General Halleck also declared that "Sherman saved the fortunes of the day on the 6th and contributed largely to the glorious victory on the 7th."

From that time Sherman was looked upon as one of the leading generals in the Army. He took part in the capture of Corinth, was commissioned Major-General of Volunteers, and in July was sent to fortify and take command of Memphis. In the siege of Vicksburg he was Grant's ablest lieutenant. For his gallant conduct he was made Brigadier-General in the Regular Army, to date from July 4, 1863. In October of that year he marched with his division to get Rosecrans out of Chattanooga, and he took part in the battle of Mission Ridge. In December he relieved General Burnside, who was hard pressed by Longstreet.

For his services at Knoxville in the Chattanooga campaign he received the thanks of Congress. The following spring he was made commander of the Military Division of the Mississippi, and moved upon Atlanta, which he captured after nearly five months of brilliant maneuvering and almost constant fighting.

He was commissioned Major-General on the 12th of August. Then he began his famous March to the Sea. His army reached Savannah, a distance of three hundred miles, in twenty-four days, and the city was easily taken.

He then turned northward, captured Charleston and Columbia, and finally received the surrender of General J. E. Johnston at Greensboro on the 14th of April, two days after Lee's surrender at Appomattox. For the terms he granted to General Johnston he has been harshly criticised, and his action was not sustained by the authorities at Washington. Undoubtedly he exceeded his authority, but it cannot be disputed that his motives were the highest.

After the close of the War, General Sherman commanded the Military Division of the Mississippi until 1869. He received the rank of Lieutenant-General on July 25, 1866. After Grant became President he was made General. He made a professional trip through Europe in 1871 and 1872. On February 8, 1884, he was placed on the retired list with full pay and emoluments.

General Sherman was the last of the great generals of the War to pass from this life. He was second only to Grant as the greatest soldier who fought on the Union side. Like Grant, he rose by his merits. His promotions were always for gallant conduct on the field of battle.

His long services in the South prior to the War might have turned the sympathies of a less patriotic man toward that section; but he believed firmly in a united country. He was one of the few men who saw at the outset the serious nature of the War, and entered the service with the full expectation that it would be a long and bloody struggle.

He dies at the allotted three-score and ten, after performing services for his country and receiving honors such as fall to the lot of few men. His is one of the names that will live in history so long as the story of the United States shall be preserved.

www.ingramcontent.com/pod-product-compliance
Lightning Source LLC
Chambersburg PA
CBHW020304170426
43202CB00008B/497